A Marine's Wife,
A Battered Life

DRESS BRUISE

A Marine's Wife, A Battered Life

DRESS BRUISE

by

Fostoria Pierson, PhD

Cover design by Michael Cooper
by direction of Author

DEDICATION

I dedicate this book to the Marine Corps, Army, Air Force, Navy, Coast Guard, Reserve, National Guard, Veterans and Veteran spouses who experienced sexual and physical abuse from the lethal hands of their Military husbands, wives or intimate partner. I dedicate this book to you if you experienced convulsive verbal abuse, psychological, and emotional abuse from any of the above mentioned Department of Defense Tenants, Homeland Security tenants or components of the Armed Forces. I dedicate this book to non-Military spouses and civilians because abuse does not discriminate. It will strip you of your self- worth, dignity, and Identity.

CONTENTS

INTRODUCTION

When I was married to Mitch, I thought my life would be secured and protected since I was part of the elite Marine Corps family. I was wrong. During the 1970s, 1980s, and 1990s, the Marine Corps did not offer adequate Family Support and Advocacy Programs to protect the spouses that were married to these "Maniac Marines." I know for sure the Marine Corps did not protect me! What you are about to read are true stories of different forms and types of abuse that we the former wives sustained while married to our Marine husbands. However, to protect the former wives that are still

1

living, the identities have been changed for their privacy and safety. The true story you are about to read is of my life as a former Marine's Battered Wife. In my narrative, the details are RAW, UNFILTERED, UNCENSORED, and SEXUAL DETAILS. This was my TRIBULATION no matter how BRUTAL and GRAPHIC. When you finish reading my story please Do not feel sorry for me because #IGOTOUT!

As I was writing my story, I called my sister Polly and said "Polly, people are going to read the deepest, darkest, and most painful secrets of my personal life as a battered wife. I don't know if I should expose it all. Polly said "Fossy if you're going to tell your story you need to be transparent. You need to tell the truth of what happened to you no matter how brutal and embarrassing. Polly said "your story might help other women and possibly

2

some men that are currently being abused. Polly was right. Sugarcoating, it will not provide the woman or man reading my story the courage or strength to leave. For years, I was too ashamed and embarrassed to tell my story, but the Lord kept it on my heart to share it. I made it OUT. Therefore, this story is not for me but for another Military or Civilian wife or Intimate partner. I have suggested to my children not to read this book. However, they are grown and should make their own decisions. My story has to be told about the abuse I withstood while married to their Marine Father. If you are currently in an abusive relationship, I pray that my story will give you a grain of courage and an ounce of strength to get out of your abusive relationship Now!

In 2005, at my small church in Virginia Beach, Virginia, some women got together for a roundtable discussion. We were asked by the Pastor to discuss a subject with each other that we had not discussed before. Eight women sat around our table in silence while glaring at each other. Finally, I spoke and said, "My Marine husband abused me for many years." I began telling my story as they listened in amazement. I felt relieved discussing my abuse openly to strangers. I was the trailblazer because other women start sharing their nightmares of the abuse they, too, were enduring or had endured even though their husbands were not military. For some of you, this will be an unsettling journal of my life to read. Foul language, traumatic episodes, sexual content and brutal descriptions are discussed. If you've never experienced abuse from your husband, wife, or intimate partner, I'm sure you know someone. What you are about to read is what I physically, sexually, and emotionally

4

suffered and encountered. Revealing my story is the only way for me to heal holistically while helping another Military Wife, Civilian Wife, Sister, Mother, or Intimate partner that is suffering in silent shame as I did for so many years. If you feel these descriptive words of physical, sexual, psychological, and emotional torture you are about to embed in your subconscious mind might offend you or are repulsive, please close this book, or pass it on to someone that needs it! I'm a Christian, and with each harsh, ungodly word I thought and wrote, I asked God to forgive me – which I believe he has because he spared my life to tell my story. Despite all the abuse, I consider myself one of the fortunate wives and Mothers because I survived. God knew I would be one of the Marine wives that lived to say #IGotOut.

If it had not been for the abuse that I endured,

I would not have been able to control my

Destiny.

Chapter 1
WHERE DID IT ALL BEGIN?

I was born Fostoria Pierson on a cold February day in Cincinnati, Ohio. I was born in the baby boomer era (1945-1965) to Father Charles Robinson and Mother Mattie Ruth Pierson. I lived with my parents, ten sisters, and one brother. I was always tall for my age, with skinny, long legs. My complexion was of a cinnamon color, and I wore my hair long. As I became older, my physique didn't change much. I was a rebellious teenager and had severe behavioral issues. I was confrontational towards my Mother, wouldn't listen to my sisters, and enjoyed being in the streets having fun and causing mischief. My father's nickname for me was "Tall 12." He named me Fostoria as well, after some small town in Ohio where he used to go fishing. I remember having a happy childhood. Even though we were destitute, we never lived in "the projects." We had clean clothes to wear, fresh bed linen and towels, but not healthy food. Some of my sisters and I were very close – and I mean as close as a knitted cap. Polly, Vanna, and I slept together in the same bed. We didn't care because we had so much fun. I was younger than the other two but much taller. My parents weren't church-going folk, but my Mother would send Polly, Vanna, and me to church with a frail white lady name Mrs. Johnson. She would come faithfully to get us for church on Wednesday evenings. We didn't mind because we got lots of delicious treats that our parents couldn't afford to buy. Most of my young life, I lived in Cincinnati, Ohio, with my siblings and parents. I remember my father waking up early in the mornings; sometimes, it was still dark. He would sit at the kitchen table and sip Lipton Tea. When my father came home in the evenings, his alcoholic beverages were Hudepohl Beer, Stroh's Beer, MD 2020, or Thunderbird, from which he would always give me sips. I could not have been any older than seven or eight years old. I still enjoy a cold beer. I would sit and watch him roll cigarettes using Bugler tobacco with thin white paper; he also smoked Camel cigarettes.

My Mother didn't work outside the home much; however, she did odd jobs cleaning and ironing for white folk. On the weekends, my Mother and Father would have friends over to the house, and they would drink Stroh's and Hudepohl Beer then dance to 45 RPM records: B.B. King, Al Green, Charles Brown, Sam Cook, and other musicians of that era. I remember my family being very stable for an extended time, then life would happen, and we would move again. During one cold winter, we packed up suddenly and moved to Ashland Street next door to the Thomas family. Mr. and Mrs Thomas a daughter Linda and son Racey. Mrs. Thomas was a beautiful woman. She reminded you of a young Lena Horne, with long hair, light-skinned, and a pop bottle shape. Mr. Thomas was tall and handsome, but he wasn't home much because he was a truck driver. Racey was a timid young man. Linda was tall, light-skinned, and very pretty, and she and I eventually became good friends.

I enjoyed staying overnight with Linda, we always had hot oatmeal, buttered toast on each side, sprinkled with sugar and cinnamon, browned in the broiler of the oven. I thought that was the best breakfast in the world! Linda was smart, and we enjoyed school, engaged in homework, and read lots of books. We were just regular kids with traditional lives, which seemed very dull to me. I had a daily routine school, homework, and outdoor playing until the street lights came on. Then, after a couple of years of living there, we moved on. We did need a bigger house with twelve kids in our family. Even though I looked forward to the move, it meant making new friends all over again. However, Linda and I remained friends. We moved to Burdette Street to a bigger house. Burdette is the street and neighborhood where I know I lost my adolescent mind. I attended Burdette Elementary School, and I was an exceptional student and looked forward to learning.

My 4th-grade teacher was an African American man name, Mr. Gaston. He would wear wire-framed glasses that set on top of his nose. He would always look over his glasses to me to make sure I was doing my school assignments, and he always challenged me academically. While in the 4th grade, he enrolled me in the local Spelling Bee with other Elementary school kids, which I did win. I was supposed to attend The National Spelling Bee in Washington, DC, but I did not want to travel on an airplane. One of the other students attended, but she lost the match. As I became older and grew into my adolescent years, I lost my mind to the adolescent hormones, which affected my way of reasoning.

Between the ages of eleven and fourteen, I became involved with the wrong group of girls: Sharone, Anna, Leslie, and Benita. These girls led me to become a female gang member. We called ourselves "The Back Stabbers" and had counterparts in the male gang members Shadey, Danny, Jimbo, and Rimp; they were "The Brady Bunch." As gang members at this early age, we fought with sticks, ropes, and brass knuckles. Most of us didn't know what guns were. We were not vicious or brutal gang members. We would fight our rival team on any given night and eat lunch with them at school the next day.

Sometimes we saved our lunch money to buy Colt 45, Schlitz Malt Liquor, Wild Irish Rose, Boone's Farm, or MD 2020 the potent 2020, not what they sell nowadays. Of course, we weren't old enough to purchase these items; however, we knew all the older kids that frequented the local Mom & Pop stores that would buy for us, or the clerks wouldn't ask for ID. Some evenings we would go to a department store called Twin Fair and steal our gang colors: blue jeans and a red bodysuit. My attitude and way of thinking were ruthless, defiant, and very aggressive during those adolescent and early teenage years. My Mom and I often had harsh arguments because I didn't want to live by her house rules. My defiant behavior towards my Mother caused a lot of strife and confrontational days with us. My Mother was ready for me to move from her house, but legally she couldn't kick me out because I was a teenager. In one of our arguments, my Mother told me if I didn't stop with my attitude and aggressive lifestyle, I would be dead before I was twenty-one. As an adolescent, I never thought I was an attractive girl, but the boys enjoyed being around me, to hang out and have fun.

One evening two of The Back Stabbers, Shadey, Danny, and I went to the store to hustle for someone to buy us some Stroh's Beer and Boone's Farm Wine to get drunk that night. Later, we went to Shadey's house because his Mom wasn't home. As we sat around getting drunk, Shadey asked me, "Have you ever had sex with two boys at the same time?" I said, "Hell, no, but I will try anything once." And I did. Shadey said, lay down, so I lay on the bed, and he got on top of me. He reeked of beer and wine. I honestly couldn't remember if his penis got hard or not because we were both so tipsy. Danny pushed him off and got on top. I just lay there with a 40 ounce in one hand sipping and sexing at the same time. I don't think any of us had an orgasm. We were thirteen and fourteen – we didn't care; we were rebellious and having fun.

When we finished having a so-called threesome, we sat on the side of the bed then realized we were out of beer and wine, so off to the store we went. We got more beer and wine then went to meet the other gang members off Woodburn Ave. Woodburn Ave was a trendy street with stores, apartment buildings, churches, and other businesses. We stood around to instigate fights with other teens that weren't in our gangs. Remember, gangs were different in the early 70s – as I said earlier, fighting with sticks and brass knuckles. Around 8:00 pm on any given weeknight, we all would go home drunk and tired and didn't care that we had school the next day. On weekends, we stayed out until 11:00 pm or after midnight to steal or start a fight. Our gang banging days went on for a few months but nothing major – just teens fighting, no drive-by shootings, stabbings, or breaking into businesses or homes. We respected older adults, and we did not vandalize our neighborhoods.

God was I the weakest link to endure such

abuse, or was I the strongest link?

Chapter 2
GIRLS JUST WANT TO HAVE FUN

When I moved from Burdette Street, which was considered Walnut Hills, we moved on Fairfax Street in the Evanston neighborhood. I met Shannon and Monica they lived directly across the street from each other, and I lived on the same street, but on another block. Monica lived next door to the Bookman's and Shannon lived directly across the street from the Bookman's. My gang banging days were over, but I continued to hang-out in the streets with different girls and boys. Shannon was not an attractive girl. She had a dark complexion,

19

big lips, short hair that she would never comb, a flat ass, huge boobs, which the boys loved. She lived with her parents Mr. & Mrs. Faggie, one sister Stephanie and one brother Yancey. Mrs. Faggie did not work outside the house, but Mr. Faggie did. He was a very jealous and insecure man and a functional drunk. The inside of their home was as dirty and nasty as a dumpsite, but Mrs. Faggie was a great cook. When Mr. Faggie came home from work, she made sure his dinner was ready, no matter what time he came back. On days that he would come from work, he would shower then a few minutes later sit at the table on which his food and beer were placed. Some days while visiting, Mrs. Faggie would come in the kitchen with a black eye, a busted lip or both. Shannon had told Monica and me that her dad got drunk and beat up her Mom. While sitting on the front porch in the evenings, Mr.

Faggie would drive up drunk then stagger into the house.

We would run to the side yard of their home then peak through the windows. After about thirty minutes, we would hear them having sex. After a few minutes he would be yelling and screaming at Mrs. Faggie if she was late placing his dinner on the table. Then, the slaps and screams would start.

Monica or I would ask, "Shannon, aren't you going inside to stop your dad from beating your Mom?" She would say, "Hell no, then I would get beat." Yancey, however, did not stand by and watch his Mom get beaten. He would jump in to help her, but his dad would beat him as well.

One summer night, while sitting on Monica's front porch, Mrs. Faggie ran out of the house, and across to where we were seated, she would cry to us to call the police. Mr. Faggie would come to drag her back across the street. These episodes would happen every weekend. I felt sorry for Mrs. Faggie, but I was just a kid and could not help her. Monica was beautiful, brown skin, deep dimples, and a lovely shape and very shy. Monica lived with her father, Mother, and seventeen siblings. Her mother, Mrs. Gooden, was as beautiful as she was. Her Mother made sure they lived in a clean house, even with eighteen kids. Mr. Gooden worked at a warehouse, and Mrs. Gooden worked part-time. Some days the Gooden's would go without eating. They would knock on the neighbor doors for food. Her oldest brother sold drugs with Lit' Jake Bookman to make sure they had food on the table. As I remember, Monica's parents didn't physically fight but did have serious confrontations. Shannon, Monica, and I were young, but we enjoyed life and wanted to have fun. We would sneak into either the

Blues club or the corner bars. Since we looked older than our age, we had older guys buying us drinks. All three of us were attracted to older men. I enjoyed the small intimate club settings. People showed so much compassion and warmth, and danced and partied all night without any confrontations – no pulling out guns or fighting. While we were at the bars, we would see Mr. Gooden. When we saw him, we would hide or sit at a corner table, so he would not see us. Each night we saw him, he was with a different woman. They would stay awhile then leave. Depending on who the woman was, they would go to her nearby apartment or go to one of the nearby motels.

He was a philanderer, and Monica knew that he had a different woman every weekend, but Monica was too afraid to tell her Mother or siblings. By midnight, Shannon, Monica, and I would stagger home; we only lived two or three blocks from the bars. When I got home, I would fight with my Mother. Remember, I was a teenager full of attitude and rebellious and didn't give a "Fuck." Monica eventually got involved with this young man that she loved, and he loved her, so she stopped hanging out with Shannon and me. Shannon and my friendship continued, and we had so much fun together for months to come.

You Wear it Well.

How is abuse supposed to be worn?

Chapter 3
NEVER SAY NEVER

While hanging out at the local high school one evening, I met Moke, a star football player, and all the girls loved him. Moke, had his eye on one girl, and that was Angel. Angel was tall, very skinny legs, medium complexion, and had dimples. She lived with her sister Benita and her Mother, who drove a bus. Angel and I became best friends. She would always come to school wearing dirty socks, and girls would make fun of her.

Moke, Shannon, and I used to hang out at an old building, drink beer, and do teenage stuff. We used to go watch Moke play football as well.

Everyone knew that he had eyes for Angel only. One football season, she and Moke start dating, after a few weeks, she became pregnant. Her Mother was so angry with her that she did not allow Moke to visit her anymore. Moke and I start hanging out. One night Moke gave me some weed to smoke, which made me paranoid and I started fighting him. I hit him in the face and broke his nose. That was the first time I ever smoked weed, and since I had a bad experience, I never smoked it again. Later I was told it was laced with LSD. As a teenager, I never used illegal drugs and never had a desire too. At least three weeks had gone by before Moke, and I saw each other at a corner store. We joked about the weed and not giving me anymore to smoke. One night instead of smoking weed, we got drunk and had sex in this abandoned building; the sex was terrible. A few weeks later, I found out I was pregnant with his child. I was stupid and trying to figure out how, because the sex was awful. Months went by, and Angel and Moke start dating again. She birthed his son, and Moke and Angel were married. In the latter part of the next year, Polly told me that Angel found out that I had a son by Moke as well and, she was not happy, and she divorced him. I was a confused single Mother with no direction in life. As months went by, I met a young man named Mitch as Shannon and I walked past his house. Mitch and his best friend Neno stopped us to invite us to Mitch's 17th birthday party, which we did attend.

Mitch lived on Fairfax Ave with his parents, Ollie and Marna Bookman, two brothers, Tance, the youngest brother and Little Jake, the oldest brother, and one sister Sinny. His grandmother Lucy owned the house in which they lived. It was a four story house that had a basement, first and second floor and an attic. Mitch was a handsome young man, light complexion, freckles, hazel eyes, and a solid build. Mitch and his family were well-known in the neighborhood. Even though I knew of this family, I did not associate with them. Mitch was known as the boy with the "bedroom eyes," and he took that literally. Rumor had it Mitch was in, and out of so many girls' bedrooms that you thought he was laying cable, somehow he was. Regardless of the rumors, Mitch and I started dating a few weeks after his birthday in June, and he introduced me to his family. His sister Sinny was married to Jon with two children, had a prosperous job, and had a great relationship with her parents. Sinny and I became good friends. Tance was gravely ill and died of Colon cancer at the age of 19. Mitch's oldest brother Lit' Jake was married to Sharren. Lit 'Jake and I knew of each other before I met Mitch. Lit' Jake drove a black car and always wore black clothes with black shades. Lit' Jake did not care for me because he knew I was aware of his dirty little secrets. He hung out on Reading Road which was a drug-infested, hooker-infested, gays and transvestites area, and he would be right in the middle of all the action. He was known as a pimp, philanderer, and a ruthless drug dealer in the surrounding neighborhoods. On weekend nights when Shannon and I would be hanging out we would see Lit' Jake with hookers standing on the corners, or with a different transvestite in his car. It was a rumor that Lit 'Jake was bisexual, and the family knew not to leave him around their boys rather kin or not. According to Mitch, Lit' Jake was traumatized by the Vietnam War. Mitch said one night while they were sleeping, Lit 'Jake woke up screaming and throwing items around, grabbing his Mother and trying to kill her. I didn't think Lit 'Jake was a kind man; maybe it was the Vietnam War that made him mean, cruel, and heartless. But I don't believe it was the War that made him a male whore and a woman beater. Lit' Jake and Sharren lived with his parents for a while. Sharren was light-skinned, huge breasts, a flat ass, and not too attractive, but intelligent. On days that I would visit Mitch I would hear and see Lit' Jake and Sharren fighting. He would punch her in the face, which left bruises, Sharren would scream stop Jake please stop! If Sharren didn't cook Lit' Jake's food the way he wanted, he would pull her by the hair then throw her to the kitchen floor. She would try to crawl away, and he would put his foot on her back or kick her. Sometimes Sharren was able to get up from the floor and run to the middle room. Sharren finally got tired of being beaten and moved in with her Mother. Lit 'Jake would bring other girls to the house that he would beat worse than Sharren, The girls he was pimping, were, slapped, punched, kicked and knocked down by him but the same girls continued to visit him. While these girls were being beat Lit' Jake's Mother and grandma Lucy would be sitting in her bedroom playing cards or dominoes and wouldn't mutter a word for him to stop. As I was watching this abuse from the stairs, I would say "Wow, I would never let a guy beat me never! One afternoon, Mitch, Sinny, and I went downtown to shop. Mitch became angry because a guy looked at me. He grabbed me by my neck and choked me, but Sinny pulled him off me while yelling at him to stop. I was crying and was so embarrassed because people were staring at us. I became so angry that I took off my shoe and threw it at Mitch.

When I got home, I went into the bathroom because I felt a burning pain on my neck. I indeed had a long bruise and scratch on my neck.

Sinny would visit her grandmother on a weekly basis. She would come in the bedroom where we all congregated. If Mitch asked me to get him a drink or something to eat and I said "No, I'm tired" Mitch slapped or punched me. Even though Sinny would intervene, the abuse continued later. She used to say, "Mitch, you are crazy; why are you still dating her if you're going to hit her?" Mitch would not respond. Sinny said "I know you love my brother, and so do I; however, you are not his punching bag." She said "My husband hit me one time, and I tried to kill him, and that Motherfucker never hit me again." Even though his sister and I got along well, I was not a selective fan of their Mothers. I spoke to his Mother several times, asking her to tell her son to stop hitting me. She would say, "Mitch, what's wrong with you? You shouldn't be hitting on her," but her words were negated by the big smirk on her fat face. Mitch and I dated for several weeks before realizing that his nickname "bedroom eyes" was accurate and that this abuse could get more severe than it had. Even though the signs were there, and he had hit me several times before, I did not want to believe that he could have traits like his mean, cruel, whorish brother. So, I allowed those thoughts and red flags to dash in and out of my mind. While Mitch and I were dating, we would stay in the attic at his grandmother's home. When Mitch didn't get his way while we were having sex, he would always slap me, but I said to myself "oh, that's not too serious." But, little did I know those slaps would turn to punches and kicks. Weeks after dating Mitch told

33

me his intensions were to date Shannon, and Neno was supposed to be my date. I knew Mitch was having sex with other girls, but I was afraid to confront him for fear of being slapped or punched, so I decided never to confront him. Honestly, I just didn't want to hear the same lies over and over again: "Baby, you know those girls don't mean anything to me. You're the girl I want to have my baby and marry." After several weeks I became pregnant by Mitch. I also heard rumors that another girl was pregnant by him as well, and we were thirty to sixty days apart, she was further along than I. Mitch, and I continued to date. I was already a teenage Mother, still living with my parents and my siblings. In March 1975, Mitch enlisted in the Marine Corps. I had my second son the latter part of April 1975. After Mitch finished boot camp at Parris Island, South Carolina, he arrived at his first duty station, Camp Lejeune, North Carolina. Even though we were not married, I visited Mitch; he asked me to marry him. I was only sixteen years old, so my Mother had to sign the documents. My Mother was so excited and relieved that I was getting married. Polly used to joke with me about how quickly Mother signed those documents and sent them back to me in Jacksonville. In September 1975, we were married. Time was going by so fast, we got married, we had two boys, and we were at a new duty station. I was so excited that I finally had a husband, but little did I know that my life would forever change, being a Marine's Wife Living a Battered Life. Little did I know that Mitch would turn out to be just like Monstrous Lit' Jake, his brother!

At times I felt like a child,

my level of abuse was based

on my behavior.

Chapter 4
LOVE DON'T LIVE HERE ANYMORE

We lived next door to a Marine family, Lorne (Marine) and wife Chasity outside of Camp Lejeune Marine Corps Base. Chasity was Italian and very thin, Lorne was white, 6'2, a slim build and they had one son. Chasity had a strong Italian accent and spoke fast. I was very naïve; I didn't know how to hang curtains, decorate my house, or make Lasagna, amongst other domestic things that a wife should know. Chasity showed me how to cook individual Italian dishes and how to do other household chores. While living next to each other, we became friends and had each other to depend on for support. While Mitch and Lorne were at work, Chasity and I would sit inside or in the front yard, drink beer, and she smoked cigarettes. If we ran out of beer or cigarettes, we would walk to the corner store to get someone to buy them. We both looked forward to when our Maniac Marine husbands were at work. We shared some in-depth emotional stories about being young Marine wives while drowning our sorrows in beer to forget about our beatings and bruises. Yes, Chasity was being abused as well. Chasity skin was of a pale color, which made her bruises very visible on her body. Sometimes she would hide them with war paint and other times she would not. I remember seeing bruises on her arms, legs, her jaw swollen, and an occasional black eye. Lorne had also broken her arm, and it was in a cement white cast. Both of us made sure we covered our bruises before our

Maniac Marines came home. If I had a bruise on my face, Mitch would say, "Fossy cover that up, I don't want to see that," while I was thinking but wouldn't say it, "but you put the bruise on my face."

On any given weekday, close to 3:00 pm/1500, Chasity and I made sure we went into the house to start cooking and our homes were neat and tidy. Every day I dreaded Mitch coming home, but the beer that I would consume made it more tolerable to put up with his shit. The beer was my liquid coping mechanism; it made me numb. It was a routine for me. After Mitch and I finished eating dinner one football Monday evening, the boys played for a little while as I cleaned the kitchen. Later, I would put the boys to bed while feeling a lot of anxiety, wondering what type of beating I would get later that evening. Mitch would drink 151 Rum and get pissy drunk, and then the sexual and physical abuse would start.

Mitch was always accusing me of sleeping with other men while he was at work. Mitch would have me go into the bedroom and undress. He would take my panties off, sniff them, or make me lie on the bed and spread my legs. He would say, "If I see anything milky or you feel wet, I will kick your ass." If he didn't see or smell anything, he would take my panties and put the crotch part in his mouth. Depending on what the scent of my panties was, or if his penis would rise, he would then push me to the bed and have me spread my legs again. Then, the nasty bastard would stick two to three of his fingers in my vagina, take it out and smell it then put it in his mouth and suck on his fingers. By that time, he was ready for sex. I would have to lie there oblivious to him while he had sex with me. As he lay on top of me, he would put his tongue in my mouth then drool in it. If I acted as though I didn't want to have sex with him or didn't want the slobber in my mouth, he would bite my nipples or stuff chocolates down my throat, taken from a box that set on the nightstand. If the beatings were horrible, I would lie in my bed crying, body too sore to move, wondering if Chasity could hear my cries and screams because sometimes I could hear hers. The walls were fragile. Chasity and I would talk the next day and Chasity would ask, "Was Mitch at it again last night? [I ask] because I heard you crying." I'd say, "Yeah." Was Lorne?" She would break down and cry. I would hear her crying out for him to stop beating her, but the beatings continued. Lorne would beat her for up to fifteen minutes. Sometimes she would run out the house and bang on our door, and he would grab her by her long stringy dark brown hair and throw her back into their duplex, she would fall on their living room floor. During the time we lived next door to each other, it seemed as though her abuse in the night lasted as long as mine. Even though my kicks to my body, punches to my face were more frequent than Chasity's.

Chasity and I always discussed ways to leave these assholes, but we were both young and inexperienced with life. I already knew my Mom would say, "You got these babies and who will help you take care of them? You need to go back to Mitch; he's a good husband he's a good father." She was half right.

One morning after Lorne went to work, Chasity knocked on my door, when I opened it she had a black eye the size of a baseball. She and I both started crying. She told me, "Fossy, I can't take this shit anymore I'm going to leave when he goes to work tomorrow." I asked, "Are you really leaving?" Chasity said, "Yeah, because love doesn't live here anymore, only beatings and bruises. I can't live like this; I have to think about my son." She and I sat on the sofa and cried because I knew that I wouldn't have a buddy to cry with or show my bruises once she left. Chasity said as we were crying and sobbing, "There's no more love in our home just misery, pain, and sorrow." After a couple of days, she was gone. She called me later and told me she was home with her Mom. Even though I looked for her throughout the years, I never heard from her again. I was sad that she was gone but happy for her because she was not being abused anymore by Lorne. But for me, I didn't have any courage, strength, or self-esteem, so I stayed – and the beatings, rape, and torture continued at least three to four days a week. Mitch had a sexual ritual with me. He came home late on a Friday night drunk as usual, and the boys were sleeping. He went into the bedroom to check on them as I sat on the sofa. Twenty minutes had passed, so I went into the bedroom, which Mitch was lying on his back across the bed. He pulled me on him as he laid there. I pushed myself up, but Mitch grabbed me towards him. He vigorously pulled off my shorts, shoved his fingers up my vagina while thrusting them for about 60 seconds, which seemed like an hour. Mitch threw me on the floor, got on top of me, and started having rough sex with me as he spread my legs apart. I cried for him to stop, but he did not. Mitch put his right hand on my throat as if he was trying to choke me, again I cried for him to stop. Somehow I was able to scurry from under him, I decided to get up and run, but he grabbed my right leg then back on the floor I fell. Mitch said, "Since that Bitch next door is gone, and you were home with just the boys who were you fucking in my bed while I was at work? I said, "Mitch, nobody." He said, "Well, I'm going to make sure you don't." Mitch punched me in my right jaw; he started hitting me in my stomach as if I was a man. I was pleading for him to stop while using my hands and arms to shield the blows. Mitch starts chuckling as if he had lost his damn mind. He then flipped me around only to bite me on my ass; it was so hard it broke my skin. I got scared, and I thought I would die that night. I cried, please, please stop you're hurting me? All of a sudden, he stopped hitting me. He sat in the chair for a second; later, he got on the bed. I finally got off the floor to go to the bathroom. There were bruises all over my stomach, my jaw had swollen, my ass was bleeding and I was in so much pain.

I showered while Mitch slept. After my shower, I went and laid on the sofa, crying silently as I always did.

What was I supposed to do?

Run away from my husband

and abandon my kids?

Chapter 5
THORNS IN THE ATTIC

Have you ever watched Flowers in the Attic? The first time I watched that movie, it was a traumatic trigger for me. It made me cry, I became angry and it brought back horrifying memories. When Mitch received orders to Okinawa, Japan, I got a reprieve. He moved the boys and me back to Cincinnati, Ohio to stay with my Mother and siblings. I felt so free and relieved that he was leaving in a few days. Since my siblings lived at my Mom's house, we stayed at Mitch's grandmother's house in the fourth-floor attic. The attic was a rectangular room with one bed, a small sofa, a TV, a VCR, a small refrigerator, and other knick-knacks. His brother Tance lived in the attic until he died. I hated the attic in his grandmother's house because it was where Mitch sodomized me, brutally raped me, and humiliated me. This particular evening, I don't know where his parents, grandmother, or Lit' Jake were, but no one was home. He bought food for me to cook dinner and bought a sexy negligee for me to wear. I knew Mitch was leaving soon, and I wanted to get my beating or torture over with for the night. I made him a Rum and coke while I only had a beer. Mitch had finished four drinks within the hour. Mitch was into rated XXX films that I thought were repulsive but had to engage for his sick pleasure. Before we started watching the nasty movie, he demanded me to put on the negligee, and he removed his clothes. As we sat on the bed watching this disgusting shit, he massaged his penis and rubbed me between my thighs. I was cringing on the inside. One nasty scene was a woman standing over the man in the movie and crapping on the man's chest, smeared it over his torso and face, then sat and glided up and down on his chest. Mitch said, "That's what I want you to do to me." I said, "Mitch, I don't have to shit, and that's disgust" before I could get the word entirely out of my mouth, he punched me in my face, which hurt like hell! Yep, you guessed it, Mitch had me stand over him, crap on his chest and play out the scene in the movie. He was fascinated with shit on his chest and golden baths-pee on his chest. He said he liked the warm feeling because it made his dick hard and would help him get off; or I would sit over his face and pee on or around it as he stuck out his tongue. Mitch was so drunk after that episode that he laid on the bed and went to sleep. Mitch enjoyed that unsavory evening, which lasted about two hours. I hated every second of it. When I went downstairs to use the bathroom, I looked in the mirror, and there was a purple and blue bruise on my right jaw, so I covered it with WAR PAINT (make-up) that I had in the medicine cabinet. About 15 minutes later, I quietly went back upstairs, praying he would not hear me. As soon as I sat on the bed, he grabbed me which startled me and I fell to the floor. He said," you thought I was finished fucking you? While on the floor, Mitch grabbed this 18-inch metal pole from the table. He roughly spread my thighs apart and said "since you couldn't get my dick hard, I want you to fuck this pole" he vigorously shoved that pole in and out of my vagina as I was screaming for him to stop. Mitch said if you scream again, I will turn you over and stick it so far up your ass it will come out your navel! While Mitch was torturing me with the pole, he dozed off on top of me a couple of times. The last time he fell asleep, he started snoring, I knew he was sound asleep, and that was my cue to get off the floor. I slowly slid my body from under his and quietly went downstairs to the bathroom.

I sat on the commode for about ten minutes sore and blood gushing out. I showered, then went into the living room and fell asleep on the sofa. Early the next morning, I heard Mitch yelling for me, which I ignored him. About 15 minutes later, he came downstairs, fully clothed, and told me to get dressed so we could leave. Mitch took us to my Mom's house and said he would pick us up at 9:00 pm. I begged, "Mitch, I want to stay at Mothers tonight." He replied, "Hell, no!" Mitch came back to get us about 9:30 that evening; then, we went to his grandmother's house. We sat downstairs with his Mom and grandmother for a while; then, Mitch told me to make a pad on the living room floor for the boys, which I went upstairs to do.

Mitch had fallen asleep downstairs in the time it took me to make the pad for the boys. He woke up, went upstairs to the attic, and I stopped to use the bathroom while praying that he would be sleep. I moved slowly, and by the time I got upstairs, he was asleep. I walked softly on the old wooden, worn-out floor so he wouldn't hear me. I quietly took off my clothes and put on my flannel pajamas mind you; it was hot as hell in the attic of thorns. I had lain down and had mixed emotions: being frightened, being nervous, and being anxious. I was lying beside him but very close to the wall and making sure that our bodies were not touching. I was praying, wishing, and hoping that he would not wake up, ever. He opened his eyes then looked at me but didn't say anything at first. Then he said, "Turn over." Damn, this Maniac Marine woke up horny. I replied, "Mitch I am so" Before I could get tired out my mouth, he grabbed my throat. He then got out of bed and dragged me to the floor while pulling both my arms. I didn't know what this Maniac Marine was going to do to me this time.

While I was lying on the floor, he forcibly spread my legs apart, got on top of me while biting on my nipples, and choked me as I was gagging; he said, "You know, I could kill you, and no one would find your body." That man had rough sex with me using the metal pole he used before. Mitch was upset because his dick was limp. This maniac sodomized me on the floor for about thirty minutes. He then tossed me on the bed to my knees, then took his belt and hit me on my Ass five or six times.

I pleaded, "Mitch, stop! It hurts!" He said, "Bitch, it is supposed to hurt." You belong to me, so turn your Ass over!" He would often say, he made it hurt now he would make it feel better. He would lick across my entire Ass with his wet, nasty tongue as he was dozing off to sleep. I could feel the saliva, which made me sick. I think after the fifth or sixth lick, he laid down and went back to sleep. After I was lying there for about ten minutes, I wondered how I could murder this bastard. I then reminded myself, "He is the property of the Marine Corps, if I kill him, I'm going to jail; then what would happen to my boys?" There were only four hours until morning. Eventually, I was able to pull my achy body out of bed and go downstairs to wash the disgust, the shame, and his Musky Maniac Marine scent off me. Then I lay on the sofa downstairs where the boys were sleeping. The year Mitch was in Okinawa,

Japan, I was ecstatic and relieved that he would be out of my life and the country for up to a year. I was so happy that I did not have to worry about being raped, sodomized, or physically abused. I met my next-door neighbor Leola, and we became good friends. She had a twin brother. Leola was a fair-skinned African American, with a flat ass and medium-size breasts and not too attractive. She used to say, "Girl, I wish I had your shape." I told Leola how Mitch abused me and how I hated him, I wish he would get killed while he was in Japan. Leola asked me, "What are you going to do?" I said, "With kids, what can I do?" While Mitch was (PCS) Permanent Change of Station I tried not to think of him. Leola and I had so much fun together. We enjoyed going to clubs. Her favorite drinks were wine coolers and Bacardi Rum and coke, and mine was 151 Rum with coke and a beer back. We would go out every weekend to nightclubs, cookouts, or some friends' homes and stay out until the early mornings. My Mom or sisters would babysit my kids. If Leola met someone, she would go home with him since she wasn't married.

Black Fred, which was his nickname, used to come get us to hang out with him, we had so much fun. But the months were winding down, and I knew Mitch was returning from Japan soon to get his family. Mitch finally came home, which Lit' Jake picked him up from the airport. I experienced many different emotions: anxiety, sadness, fear, as adrenaline raced through my body every second. I did not want to be with Mitch as his wife anymore; I hated this man. But what kind of stable financial life could I provide for my boys and myself? I had to mentally convince myself that he would be a changed man, reminding myself, "He is your husband, and he has been away for almost a year, so try to make the best of it." The night he came home he asked me to have my Mom watch the boys, which she did. I thought, "A night without the kids – maybe we would go to a movie or dinner "Nope, we went to his brother Lit' Jake's house, even though Mitch knew his brother and I did not like each other." While at Lit' Jake and Sharren's home, we sat around and sipped on beer and wine, which Lit' Jake did not drink alcohol, and Mitch had 151 Rum and coke. Mitch and Lit' Jake were at the kitchen table talking, and Sharren and I were sitting on the sofa. We heard them talking about other women, and Sharren and I just looked at each other and shook our heads. Sharren walked over to the kitchen to get more wine, and Lit' Jake asked "What the fuck are you over here for?" She replied, "More wine." He said, "Bitch, if you don't get your ass back on the sofa, I will kick you over there." After about an hour, Mitch and Lit' Jake "went for a ride, "this is what Lit' Jake always did when he'd go pimping girls. While they were gone, Sharren and I sat talking for at least three hours then they returned. Mitch said, "Let's go," so I got up, hugged Sharren, then we went back to "Thorns in the Attic." We stopped on the way to buy White Castles which we ate them before we arrived home. When we got out of the car, Mitch told me to use the bathroom but not shower and go upstairs. I was trembling and scared but did as he demanded. I don't know what was stirring in Mitch's freaky and demented mind, but I knew it wasn't pleasant. When we got to the attic, Mitch made me stand up while he tied me to a fixture that was attached to the ceiling. Next, he unbuttoned my blouse and pulled off my skirt. My arms extended up, and my legs spread apart. I'm shaking uncontrollably thinking, "What in the hell is he going to do to me?" Mitch took some whipped cream and sprayed it all over my body front and back; he drew circles and shapes in the foam. Then he put his mouth over my right nipple and started nibbling it, then the left one which he rotated back and forth for about two minutes, which seemed like twenty minutes. He began to lick the cream off the front of me. I cried out loud on the inside but silently on the outside because I did not want to make him angry. Mitch spread my legs apart and put his entire face in my Ass while making sounds as if it were tasty. He turned me the other way and put my legs across the bed as he took his face and smudged it between my thighs. Next, he came up to me and jolted his dick in my vagina as hard as possible then removed it. He then lubed the metal object with whip cream and lunged it in my vagina so hard that

I trembled and cried while pleading with him to stop. He said, "stop," that son of a bitch punched me so hard on the right side of my face that I had a headache for the rest of the night. Mitch began wiping the cream off my body only to urinate on me. The disgusting sexual acts that he did to my body were humiliating. Mitch always had loud music playing, so no one could hear my cries, yells, or screams. Mitch knew his Mother or father would not come up to the attic even though their room was beneath it. Behind closed doors, Mitch was a maniac, a freak, and a monster. "Was I going to make it out alive that night, I did not know?" Mitch wanted to make sure that I didn't leave or kill him, so he tied me to the bed with one of his black socks then went to sleep. The next morning, when we woke up, he untied me and said he was going to visit his brother, which he was gone for hours. His sea bag with clothes, shoes and his medical record were on the floor. I looked through it but not looking for anything in particular. To my surprise, Mitch had contracted a Venereal Disease from one of the Okinawan women. Did I confront him? "No, being beaten, battered, and bruised, I learned to pick my battles – at least that's what I thought." Mitch's best friend Neno had come over to visit Mitch one evening before going to his next duty station. Neno had told him I had been hanging out with Moke again, which I said was not true, but he didn't believe me. If I forgot to mention it, it was Neno's sister that Mitch had impregnated, but he denied her infant daughter. I was at my Mother's house with our boys when Mitch came over. He pulled up, so I walked out to the car, got inside, and sat down. As soon as I sat, the Motherfucker punched me so hard in my face I jumped out the car ran around the car to the front side of the house. He jumped out and ran around and caught me. He grabbed me and held my head between his hands then slammed it against my Mother's brick house. I swear I felt my brain shift. He said, "You fucking ho! I heard you were fucking Moke again, and I am taking care of his fucking son." I was sobbing and crying, I said, "Mitch, that's not true, and my head is hurting, you need to take me to the doctor." He said, "I'm not taking you anywhere, and you're going to die tonight." I said, "Mitch, please stop!" He punched me in my chest, pushed me to the ground and kicked me. Somehow, I got up and away from him and ran into the house. My Mom asked me what was wrong, and I told her Mitch had hit me again. My Mom said, "You all need to stop it with that stupid shit, get in there and take care of those babies." Mitch pulled off as I was lying on the bed, my head hurting and a bluish-black bruise on my chest which I didn't go to the hospital, I covered it with War Paint. I stayed at Mother's home that night, afraid of going to the attic I didn't feel like being beat and raped. Leola came over the next day; she asked me if Mitch was home. I said "yes" and told her that Mitch's lying friend told him I was hanging out with Moke, and he punched me and banged my head against the house. She asked if I told my Mom. I said, "Yeah, but what could she do, what could anybody do?" Leola was brutally killed by her boyfriend's nephew a couple of years later. He tried to rape her. While trying to fight him off, he overpowered her, knocked her unconscious, raped her, and set her body on fire. The autopsy showed "she was still alive while her body was in flames." Years later, the guy that murdered her was killed.

I prayed for my beatings...

I prayed this one wouldn't be as bad as the last

one.

Chapter 6
SAVED BY THE BELL

Mitch had PCS (Permanent Change of Station) to Marine Corps Air Station El Toro, California in 1979. His brother Lit Jake came to Camp Lejeune to help him drive cross country. We had three boys and one of them was 3 weeks new. Since base housing wasn't ready, we stayed with my Gay brother Sylvester in Los Angeles for a few days. Mitch went to check in with his unit and put us on the waiting list for base housing. Lit' Jake and my brother appeared to be attracted to each other. Sylvester made comfortable pads for us to sleep on the floor. However, in the middle of the night, Lit' Jake disappeared from the floor pads. Mothers know "With a three-week old baby you don't get any sleep!" I heard moaning and squeaking. I walked past Sylvester's bedroom on the way to fix my infant son a bottle of Similac Formula. I peaked in the cracked opening of the bedroom door and Sylvester and Lit' Jake was in a Leap Frog position on his king-size bed. Sylvester was humping Lit' Jake. I hurried to the kitchen to heat the formula before my son was fully awake, and they heard me in the kitchen. After staying a few days with my brother, Mitch decided we would move to the Hostess House (base hotel) closer to the base. Weeks later, we were called for base housing and moved in within days. The year was 1979; we had the boys with us which our youngest son was then a month old. Once settled in, we soon met other

66

married Marine couples: San and Ken; Barra and Charles; Rhonda and Mick; Freda and Hennison; Pamela and Jonas, Deidra and Floyd and others. San was a beautiful Creole, and Ken was an okay looking brown-skinned guy. San had found what she was looking for – a man to take care of her and her daughter. Mitch and Ken became best friends as well as Hennison and Mitch. Barra and Charles were our Puerto Rican friends. Barra and I became friends and we worked at the Commissary together. Mitch and Charles were just hi and bye buddies.

The other Marines were card and Dominoes buddies. Some of our outings with other Marine families were playing cards, dominoes, cookouts, and birthday parties for our kids or the adults. After a while, this got boring to me, and I wanted to get a job. I applied for a job at MWR (Morale Welfare Recreation) and was hired as an assistant manager for the Tustin Base bowling center, even though we lived at base housing on El Toro. It was a straight path, and less than twenty minutes away. Each time I would come to work, I would drive through the main gate where there were Military Police that would check your Military ID card before granting you access to the base. Each time I drove through the gate, this MP Lance Corporal Neil, would be at the entrance to wave guests on. Sometimes he would take my ID card and keep it longer than usual before he allowed me to enter the base. One summer day, I drove through the gate, and he wasn't on duty. I was working that night and had to close the bowling center, which was small – I think about eight lanes. That night LCpl Neil came into the bowling center and walked over towards me as I helped another Marine and his family. He waited until I finished, then he walked over and asked what time I got off work. I told him 2300/11:00 p.m. He told me he wanted us to go on a date. I said, "I'm married; I can't go out with you." He said, "Really? Your husband doesn't think he's married." He asked me was I married to Corporal Bookman. I said, "Yes. How do you know?" "Because he works on this base, and don't you guys live over here." I said, "No." He said, "Oh when I patrol the housing areas, I always see his car parked on the Cul-de-sac with the same woman." "He's probably visiting one of his Marine families," LCpl Neil said "I don't think so because sometimes I patrol at 0200/2:00 a.m. and his car is there. He drives a brown Cadillac, right?" I answered in the affirmative he then asked me to go on a date with him again. I replied, "My husband would kill me if he even saw me speaking to you." It was time for me to lock up because the last customer left at 2300/11:00 pm. I mentioned to LCpl

Neil that an MP always came through to make sure the building was secure after I exited, and he said, "I know, I already took care of that; the MP is me tonight." There was no computer cash registers, so I hand counted the money in the drawer to cash out. I inventoried the food, snacks, and beer. The lanes had to be swept, LCpl Neil offered to clean the lanes. I went behind each machine to make sure no bowling balls were stuck and set correctly. After we finished, I asked if he wanted a beer, so we sat and had a couple of beers. It was 2345/11:45 pm. I said, "It's time for me to go because Mitch is going to start wondering where I am." LCpl Neil said, "No, he's not." I asked "How do you know?" "The MP is patrolling that area, and he told me that Mitch's car is at that same house tonight." I said, "Really, I'm so tired of him and his whorish shit." LCpl Neil said, "You got me, sweetheart." LCpl Neil walked toward me and started kissing me on my lips, my neck then took off his shirt, laid it on lane number three, and gently laid me on it. Honestly, I didn't know what to do; I was scared. It felt so good to lie with a man without getting punched, raped, or slapped. The next thing I knew, he started kissing me on my breast, then down my stomach, he lifted my legs and licked me so sensually on each thigh, going from one thigh to the other. I felt something so wet and warm licking on my vagina while kissing it so sensually. I had never felt a man make love to me as he did. After about twenty minutes of making love to me with his mouth, he slowly brought himself on top of me and inserted his penis and "OMG!" I said to myself, "Not only is he a fine Marine, but he is also a Mandingo Marine." It was 2400/12:00 a.m. I got dressed and told LCpl Neil I had to go, because Mitch should be home by now, and he would be upset if I weren't home when he got there. LCpl Neil told me he was not home yet because the MP would let him know when Mitch was leaving. "Believe me, I don't want you to get in any trouble," LCpl Neil added. I said, "Trouble, you just don't know how much." LCpl Neil asked what did I mean; I said "nothing." LCpl Neil and I left out at the same time, by the time I got home, it was 0100/1:00 a.m., and Mitch wasn't back yet. I took a shower and went to bed.

I woke up around 0645/6:45 a.m. and Mitch still wasn't home, so I lie back down until about 0900/9:00 a.m. When I woke up, the boys were in the kitchen with Mitch. He had cooked breakfast and they were sitting at the kitchen table eating then the boys went into their bedroom after they finished. I asked Mitch if he had duty last night, he said, "Yeah, you know I told you I did." I bravely said, "No, I don't remember you telling me." I asked him, "So why was your car parked on Tustin Drive last night?"

"Ken dropped me off where I had duty; he kept my car because he had to take San to work." I said, "Mitch, you're lying, 'cause San doesn't work." He said, "Are you calling me a liar?" I was answering in the affirmative, then he punched me in my stomach, grabbed my neck and yelled, "Don't you ever call me a liar again." I was so STUPID! After all the previous beatings, I still didn't know how to choose my damn battles! Standing there hurting and in fear, I waited until he left, then I went in my bedroom to lay down, crying my dumb heart out and wondering why me? Later that night, when Mitch came home, he had a dozen red roses and a box of chocolates in his hands. I was sitting on the couch, and he walked towards me and sat next to me and said, "Fossy, I am so sorry, and that will never happen again, I promise." Two or three days went by, and Mitch came home drunk as usual. He came into the kitchen while I was cleaning. Then came the hammer blow: Mitch said, "Yeah, I found out you're messing with that MP at the gate. I wondered why each time I came through the gate, he always looked at my Military ID for a period of time then he'd stare at me once he waved me through." "Mitch, we are not messing around." He said, "Come on get dressed." When I asked where we were going, he said, "To the gate to see your boyfriend." I said, "He's not my boyfriend!" Then I tried reasoning, "What about the boys?" He said they would be okay until we got back. I got in the car, and I was scared of what would happen when we got there. Thank God, LCpl Neil was off duty. Mitch asked the Sergeant at the gate where MP

LCpl Neil was, and he replied: "at the office." So, we drove over to his office, and Mitch forced me to get out of the car and go inside with him. When we went inside, LCpl Neil was standing at the desk, Mitch said, "So, you're fucking my wife." Neil said, "Man, what are you talking about?" Mitch said, "I need to speak to your Gunny." Neil went and got the Gunny. When Gunny came out of his office, Mitch said, "Gunny, your LCPL is messing with my wife." When the Gunny asked LCpl Neil if this was true, of course, he said, "Hell, no!" Gunny said, "He denies it." Mitch looked at LCpl Neil and said, "You better stay away from her, or you will be sorry." Well, I knew who would be sorry. I was walking alongside Mitch when we got out of the MP building; Mitch back slapped me so hard with his arm across my upper torso that I thought my clavicle had cracked. When we pulled up at home, I cried because I didn't want to go inside the house. I knew what would happen. I took my time getting out of the car, and he said, "If you don't move a little faster, I will drag your fucking ass inside." Mitch made sure I walked in front of him so, I wouldn't run away. As soon as we got into the small foyer of the house, Mitch kicked me from behind, and down to the floor I went. He jumped on top of my back and shouted, "Oh, you want to fuck this MP, huh!" He punched me on the right side of my face he jumped up and grabbed me by the back of my shirt to lift me, walked a few feet, then slung me into the bedroom door, which jingled the bell that hung on the doorknob. He then pushed me towards the bed, but I fell on the floor he started kicking me on my right side. I lay there praying and crying that he would not kick me anymore. Mitch exited the bedroom for a few minutes to check on the boys.

When he returned, he snatched my blouse off; he proceeded to pull my shorts and panties off vigorously. After he got my clothes off, he got on top of me and shoved his penis in me as hard as he could and started raping me while saying, "Fuck me like you fucked that MP!" He was biting and slapping me back and forth from the right side of my face to the left. He was punching me in my chest repeatedly as King Kong punches himself in the chest. I was begging and crying for him to stop, but he did not. The torture would have lasted longer than it did if it had not been for one of the boys who heard my cries and knocked on the door. The knock rang the bell that hung on the outside doorknob to our bedroom. I was relieved as I was praying, and my entire body was in so much pain. I was thanking God that I was literally "Saved By the Bell. "After that night of being brutally beat once again, I did not see LCpl Neil anymore, nor did I enter that side of the gate where he patrolled to get to work. One thing I know for sure. When I die, there is only one place my soul can go and that is Heaven. I never knew what the phrase "beat the hell out of meant" until it happened to me that evening #IGOTOUT.

If it had not been for the abuse in my life, I would not have accomplished something that I have never done before and I would not have made it to my destiny!

Chapter 7
STOMP

My name is Polly sister of Fostoria (Fossy), which I am a couple of years older than she. My young son and I went to live with Fossy in the spring of 1980 when she was pregnant with her twin daughters. Late June, my son's father came to take him to Georgia to visit him. Since he was gone, I decided to get a job at the Marine Corp Exchange. In between my work schedule, I would help my sister with her kids and house chores. While living with my sister, I remember her always looking fatigued, somber, and depressed. She would very seldom comb her long pretty hair or put on clothes. I remember Mitch being cruel and often said demeaning things to her. Mitch wasn't one of my favorite brothers-in-laws. He was verbally and physically abusive to Fossy, and he drank too much which contributed to her depression. During this visit, I only stayed for a few weeks then I went back to Cincinnati. I had only been home for several weeks when our Mother received a call from the American Red Cross. The message was that Fossy was sick, and Mother needed to come to take care of the kids since she would be admitted to the hospital on the Psychiatric ward. Our Mother could not go, so I went back to California to help with the kids so Fossy could get the help she needed. Mitch didn't want me there to help her. He kept saying she was lazy and didn't want to take care of the kids. Mitch drove Fossy to the hospital; I didn't want her to go, but I knew she needed professional help. Even though he was cruel to my sister, he appeared to be a good father. Fossy was in the hospital for at least three weeks. I would get the older boys ready for school, and the other kids stayed home with me. Mitch was gone all the time when Fossy was in the hospital. I think he was having an affair. In the mornings, Mitch wore Cammies to work, when Mitch came home in the late evenings, he had on civilian clothes, was drunk and smelled of cheap perfume. Some nights he called to check on the kids but didn't come home. Mitch didn't want me there, and he even told me on several occasions to go home, and I told him, "Not as long as my sister is in the hospital."

While living with my sister and family in base housing, I met Omar's wife, Sana. They lived in the housing area where Fossy and Mitch lived. She knew Mitch hung out with Omar and other Marines. Sana and I became best friends and started hanging out at the NCO clubs, the Exchange, or the Marine Barracks. Even though she was married, she would disappear in barrack rooms to have sex with different Marines. I'd sit in the car and wait until she finished or go home to check on the kids then go back to get Sana. One night as we were sitting outside watching the kids play, she said, "You know Mitch is a 'ho." I said, "Mitch, who?" She said, "Fossy's husband." I asked her how she knew. She said, "I heard rumors that he was sleeping with other Marine wives when their husbands were deployed." I shared I knew something was going on because Fossy was so unhappy. That's another reason why I don't like his cheating Ass. The kids missed their Mom so much. I knew she was experiencing something that I just couldn't put my finger on. Three weeks later, Fossy came home from the hospital. She appeared to be very sluggish and in a zombie state of mind. Mitch didn't like Fossy being drugged so four days after she came home from the hospital, he threw away her medicines. I felt so sorry for her because there was nothing I could do to help her. She had to cope with whatever she was going through with Mitch the best way she could. Hennison was another one of Mitch's Marine buddies, and he was married to Freda. Weeks went by, and Fossy was feeling better and was starting to get some energy. She and Mitch began to act like a married couple. One evening they went out to eat and to a movie. Fossy: Mitch phoned Hennison, and they decided the four of us would go to the Staff NCO Club on Camp Pendleton. Hennison and Freda came to our house, listened to some music, and had some adult beverages before we went to the club. We all felt good that night, and I had on this beautiful yellow dress that buttoned down the front, I knew I looked good. When we got to the club, we sat at a table which was up against the wall. The music was old school and sounding good. The ambiance of the room was dark, but with just enough light to dance. Freda and I sat while Mitch and Hennison went to the bar to get us a drink. We danced song after song and were having a funky good time. Then, my smiles went to frowns. Mitch had five too many drinks. As Freda and I were on the floor dancing, Mitch came to the floor and grabbed me. Hennison was still sitting at the table, and he just sipped his non-alcoholic drink and pretended as though he didn't see anything. Mitch pushed me in the chair against the wall and pinched my arm hard enough to break my skin. Mitch tilted the chair then pushed me to the floor he leaned down to shove me under the table. Since our table was up against the wall no one could see or noticed what happened. The music was loud, hands were clapping, and fingers were popping. I was crying out loud, but no one could hear me. As I sat under the table, Mitch was kicking me as if I was a damn dog. He stomped on my right hand with his right foot as my hand was flat on the floor. I grabbed his right leg to bite it as Mitch kicked me with his left foot. I tried to crawl from under the table, and that asshole kicked me in my upper torso area. I stopped fighting him as I bent over in pain. Freda came to the table and must have asked where I was. Due to all the noise and music she could not have heard my screams. I assumed Mitch or Hennison must have told her I was under the table. "Freda looked under the table and saw me, and she started cussing at Mitch and

Hennison. Hennison said, "It's none of your damn business, so be quiet before I put your fat Ass under there." I sat under that table, crying and so humiliated for about an hour. As they were packing up to leave the club, Mitch pulled me up by my hair and sat me in the chair. He made me fix my dress as it was twisted. Hennison was sitting there and did not say a word to Mitch or ask if I needed any help. We proceeded to leave the club, as we walked through the long foyer (hall), other Marines and spouses looked at how forcefully he was holding my arm but did not offer me any help. Mitch slapped me so hard once we got in the car that I saw floating stars, he said, "Wait until we get home." Hennison and Freda fussed and cussed at each other all the way home, Hennison put Freda in a chokehold. She was gasping for air and crying. We dropped them off at their car, then we went into our home; we only lived a few minutes away from each other. Polly: I heard the door open about 0200/2:00 a.m. then I heard Mitch cussing. The next thing you know, the bedroom door shut. I didn't hear anything because the TV was loud, so I went to sleep. The next morning I saw Fossy she had a bruise the size of an egg on the right side of her face.

Fossy: Mitch beat me with a belt; sodomized me with a cucumber. Mitch removed the cucumber from my vagina, while forcibly trying to open my mouth while I'm gasping for air. He overpowered me and thrust the cucumber in my mouth. While the cucumber was in my mouth, Mitch was chanting suck it Bitch, suck it! He was making some disgusting sounds. Mitch said, "I'm going to fuck you with my fingers" that Bastard forced his fingers into my vagina twisted and turned them for at least

15 minutes. Mitch tried forcibly to put that cucumber in my ASS somehow I did a Donkey back kick into that Bastard's chest, so he stopped! While being tortured, I beat this Motherfucker on every inch of his upper body, but he did not feel any of my punches with all the liquor in his bloodstream. Mitch took a belt and hit me all over my body. This torture went on for up to two hours. When the torture was finally over, every inch of my body was in agony. I was exhausted, in agonizing pain, and was humiliated. Mitch fell asleep quickly as he always did. While Mitch was sleeping, I laid there in intense pain. I dragged my painful body into my garage to load my gun. I was crazed out of my mind. While trying to load my gun, I was so nervous I dropped the bullets. I walked across the kitchen floor, making a noise that awakened Polly. I walked into the bedroom and stood over Mitch while he was

lying on his back butt-naked. I had the gun pointed at the tip of his head and not the head attached to his neck. Polly walked in as she heard me cock the gun; she was crying and begged me not to kill him. I explained, "Polly, I am tired of being beaten by this man; he stomped me as if I was a dog while we were at the club." Polly: "Please think about your kids; you will go to jail, the Marine Corps won't help you; please don't kill him." Fossy: We went into the living room, and we talked, and Polly asked if she could get some ointment to rub my body. I said, "No." We cried and discussed how I could leave him within minutes we fell asleep.

God, I always felt you had forsaken me,

but then I realized: you gave me your word, and

you knew I would be alright.

Chapter 8
BLUE SEQUINED GOWN

It was October, and the Marine Corps Ball was in November. Ora called me to ask which day I wanted to go shopping to find a gown for the Ball. I told her any day would do. She said, "Let's go during the weekday," which we did. We went to several stores and looked at several gowns. After about three hours of shopping, Ora finally found this beautiful Royal Blue Sequins gown for me to wear. She told me to come early afternoon the day of the Ball so she could make up my face. I said, "Ora, you know the only time I wear war-paint is when I have to hide a bruise or a black eye." Her response was, "I'm sorry, Nyno, but please let me make up your face for the Ball. I have this beautiful wig you can wear also." Nyno was a nickname that Ora called me. I arrived to Ora's house at 1300/1:00 p.m. By the time I got there, Ora already had different make-ups selected for my skin-tone. She started applying three to four different types of make-up on my face, which made me look beautiful. She covered the bruise that was in its healing stage. Ora asked, "Is Mitch still hitting you?" I said, "Yeah, and I just don't know what to do." She suggested that I "kill that Motherfucker," we joked about me killing him. I said, "Ora, I can't go to his command because he already threatened me. If I tell someone, my friends will tell their husbands; then Mitch will find out." I stayed until she finished applying my make-up, then I went home. On the outside, I looked gorgeous! I was grateful that God didn't give us X-ray eyes. Because with X-ray eyes, anyone who looked at me would have seen; my heart shattered like glass; my emotional trauma scrambled in my head like eggs; my intangible pain that draped my weary, achy body like water flowing from a waterfall. Mitch and I went to the Ball around 1800/6:00 that evening. I was looking forward to having a great time because I always loved to dance, socialize, and just have fun. We listened to the Marine Corps presentation, ate dinner, drank champagne, danced, and conversed with other Marines and their wives. We had been there at least two hours when Mitch asked me to step out in the foyer. I followed him over towards a corner while anxiety raced through my body as I thought, "I know this bastard is not going to punch or slap me in front of all these Marines and their wives, thank God," He did not. Instead, Mitch grabbed my right hand and bent back my fingers; then, he pinches me underneath my forearm. I asked, "Mitch, what is wrong? What did I do?" He said he saw the Sergeant Major and me looking at each other; I said, "Yeah, Mitch, we spoke." He said it looked like something else, and I assured him it wasn't. We stayed at the Ball for another forty-five minutes, but my fun had ended. Mitch said, "Let's go, and make sure you get some cake." I was puzzled and asked, "Why? You don't eat cake." He just rumbled, "Didn't I tell you to get some fucking cake?" I walked over to the table and cut five pieces to give the kids some the next day. We said goodbye to the other Marine couples and exited the ballroom. As we walked to our car, the Motherfucker tripped me. I fell to the ground and the wrapped slices of cake. I skinned my elbows, thank

God I had on a long gown, or I would have skinned my knees. I picked the cake up and got in the car. Mitch started driving home; the first ten minutes, we did not speak. He then asked me what was going on with the Sergeant Major and me. I repeated nothing was going on, Mitch back-slapped me so hard across my face the earring I was wearing dropped in my lap, and my nose started to bleed. I said, "Mitch, please don't start hitting me again." He responded, "Oh, just wait till we get home!" As Mitch was driving home, I planned to jump out the moving car. When Mitch pulled up to a stop sign, I pulled the door handle to jump out, he grabbed me and the car swerved as other drivers were looking on. Then Mitch stopped the car and yelled, "Are you fucking crazy? What are you trying to do kill yourself?" I answered, "I'd rather kill myself than let my kids grow up knowing that their father beat me to death!" Ten minutes later, we pulled up at home. When we arrived, the kids were asleep. I put the cake on the kitchen counter went straight into the bathroom to clean off my elbows. Mitch came into the bathroom, grabbed my head, and started slamming it against the bathroom door. He had not changed out of his Dress Blues. He said, "Get your Ass out that gown." As soon as I removed the gown from my body Mitch grabbed it, went into the kitchen, got a pair of scissors, and cut my Blue Sequins gown into pieces. I was in the bedroom by the time he came back with the gown pieces which he threw at me. He said, "Now you want the Sergeant Major to see you in this gown; take it to him, you fucking ho!" I pleaded my innocence, he said, "Well, I'm going to make sure he sees you in black and blue!" Mitch punched me in my mouth. After Mitch punched me, I went back into the bathroom and locked the door to wash the blood from my mouth. He then banged on the door and yelled, "Unlock this fucking door before I kick it in." I unlocked it, and after a few minutes, I walked into the bedroom. He came towards me, raising his fist to hit me, I blocked his hits and cried, "Mitch, please don't, I am so tired of you hitting me." He said the words that most abusers say, "Why do you make me do these things to you?" He grabbed me by my arm and twisted it very hard. I thought he would break it. Then, he pushed me up against the wall. I was crying for him to stop, but he wasn't listening. He threw me on the floor and kicked me in my side with hesitation as if he knew he might break a rib or something. He unbuttoned his Blues Coat and unzipped his pants but didn't remove them right away, he kicked off his shoes. Mitch yelled," I have control over you bitch." I got off the floor and onto the bed. Mitch slid the Khaki belt from his blues pants and hit me with it a couple of times. Again, what could I do? He said, "Lay your Ass across the bed, you want to fuck the Sergeant Major, so you say his name while I'm fucking you." When I wouldn't say the Sergeant Major's name because I didn't know it, Mitch bit me on my nipples, ears and punched me again in my mouth. As I was crying for him to stop, he said, "No, I'm going to fuck you till you say his name." So I uttered his rank, "Sergeant Major," Mitch then said, "So you do want to fuck him, huh." Mitch got the slices of cake, stuffed them down my throat, and smeared them in my face and body.

Mitch continued to rape me in between beating me on my back with his Khaki belt. After he finished, I crawled into the bathroom and sat in the corner to rest before getting in the bathtub. I was too sore from being beat to lift my legs to get in. I eventually looked in the mirror and saw that I had black and blue scars over my body, and I needed to Dress those Bruises. The next morning was Sunday, and I could hear the kids in the other room, playing and watching TV. Mitch had finally got his drunk, stinky Ass out of bed and went to get a beer out of the refrigerator. I laid there in a gaze and pain while staring at the ceiling. I wondered what in the hell did I do in my young life to deserve this Abuse. My life was over, and I indeed was going to die at the hands of this Maniac Marine. What could I do? Who could I trust to share about my Abuse? These words always echoed in my mind: "Don't go to my command." I was a Marine's wife surviving a battered life. I Wore It Well Because No One Could Tell!

God, Was I the weak Marine's wife

or the chosen Marine's wife?

Chapter 9
GET OUT

On this particular quiet evening, I was not feeling well in my head. As Mitch slept, I sat in the dark, staring at him for hours, wondering, "When were the beatings going to end?" I knew the Marine Corps would not help me. I got up in a daze, went in the kitchen, got my cast iron skillet, filled it with oil, and heated it on the stove. As the oil was getting hot, I went into the kids' rooms, wrapped them in blankets, put them in the car, started it, and turned on the heat. I sat in the driver's seat for a while, crying when one of the boys woke up and asked if I was okay. I said, "Yeah, Mommy's just cold and tired." Several minutes passed, so I went into the kitchen to remove the heated oil off the burner with a hand mitt. I was in such a daze I don't remember if I turned off the stove. Still, in my trance, I walked back into the bedroom as Mitch was lying on his back, snoring. I tilted the skillet while pouring the hot oil onto his torso then I dropped the black cast iron skillet on his chest. Mitch let out the most horrifying screams and yells – more horrific than mine when he would torture me. I turned away and strolled out of the house to my car, drove to my girlfriend Barra and Charles' house. When I got there, I knocked and banged on the door until Barra opened the door as Charles slept. I was crying hysterically and telling Barra I just couldn't take another beating or be raped by Mitch again. My body was physically worn out, and my mind was emotionally exhausted. She asked, "Fossy, what happened, and where are the kids?" I said, "In the car," then I told her what Mitch did. She asked where he was; I replied, "Home." Barra went into the kitchen and used the phone (landline) to call him, which I didn't want her too.

Barra: Mitch answered and told me that he had called an ambulance. I heard voices in the background. After we put two of the kids on the sofa and the other three upstairs, Fossy and I got into the car to go to the hospital. I don't remember if she drove or I. Once we got to the hospital, which was not a Military hospital Fossy told me to tell the nurse that I was his sister. We went to the front desk to ask for him and I told the nurse that I was Barra Booker, his sister, so she let us go in. As we walked into his room, the nurses and doctors were working on Mitch. To me, he did not look well. Fossy looked as though she started feeling sorry for him so she went out to the lobby. I went back to ask Mitch what he did to her, and he said, "Hit her." I told him that was wrong. I was scared that night because Fossy didn't look normal – she looked almost out of her mind. I had never seen her like that before. She was always laughing and having fun. After we got back to my house, it was almost the break of dawn, so the kids and Fossy went back home. I went over the next day to strip the bed down of the soiled oily linen.

Fossy: After a day or so, I took the kids to see their father. He was not awake because the doctors sedated him since he was in so much pain. He was lying in the burn unit bandaged but I did not feel sorry for Mitch. I wanted him to feel some physical pain and suffering that I felt for so many years; and I wanted him to die. Mitch was in a lot of pain, and tears were visible from his face. I ignored his tears just as he always ignored mine. While Mitch lay bandaged in the hospital, this was my time to get out. I felt as though I was at the end of my supply line of life and couldn't hold on much longer. I had so much hatred, bitterness, and anger in my heart for Mitch. I felt as though I was out of my mind and trying to save my life. A few weeks later, Mitch came home from the hospital, which I had to take care of him. Mitch cried and cried that he was so sorry and he would never beat or rape me again. Dumb Ass me, I started feeling awful about what I had done to him. Over the next several weeks, I rationalized in my mind that he would be different. Maybe this horrific incident scared him straight, and he wouldn't abuse me anymore. I sincerely wanted to believe him and that our marriage would be better – that he would be a different man, husband, Marine. Gullible me, stayed, while trying to figure out if the kids and I escaped from him, how would I make it financially? Who would hire me? What or whom would be my security blanket? Mitch eventually got orders to Camp Pendleton because (BRAC) Base Realignment and Closure closed El Toro, Marine Corps Air Station.

The proof that I had gone to War but lost the Battle, were the scars, bruises, and black eyes that I walked away with.

Chapter 10
EVERY SHUT EYE AIN'T SLEEP

I had come home from work one late summer evening. Mitch was either at work or in some woman's bed. I cooked dinner, took a bath, and then laid down to rest. I heard a noise that woke me; it was 8:30 p.m., and the kids were in the other room watching TV. I looked through-out the house, and Mitch wasn't home yet, so I went to lie back down. He came in about 30 minutes later and said hi to the kids. He came into the bedroom, and I just lay there and pretended to be asleep while he changed his Cammies. Mitch said, "I'm going to my part-time job," which was at the Arco gas station in Oceanside, California. After Mitch left, the kids went to their rooms, and I cleaned the kitchen and then sat to watch TV. Then, at 10:30 p.m., the home phone rang. I answered it, and it was a woman on the other end. She asked, "Is this Mitch's wife?" I said, "Yes. She said, "This is Carolyn, and I'm fucking your husband," I said, "Yeah, you and all the other whores he's screwing. How did you get my number?" She said, "He gave it to me." I asked, "Why are you calling me," Carolyn said Mitch told her we were separated and getting a divorce? I said, "Girl, we have been separated many times, and I keep taking his no good whorish Ass back. You have to be the 10th or 11th girl he's been messing around with, but honestly, I lost count. What do you want?" Carolyn said, "Well, I work at this convalescent home behind Arco, and Mitch brings me lunch at midnight, so if you want to confront him, be here about 12:05 a.m." I asked, "What for if you and he are dating?" She said, "Well, I think he's been lying to me." I responded, "No shit Sherlock! He's been lying to me for years, and I'm his damn stupid wife, so why should you be any different?" I agreed to go to her job. So, I lay back down, thinking about how this son-of-a-nasty-bitch was at it again. It was about 11:45 p.m. when I headed to her job. Just like she said, Mitch pulled in the parking lot around midnight he got out of the car carrying a plastic bag. When I saw this short, fat, black female walk toward him, I sat there in amazement for a few seconds, thinking, Damn, I'm not a Tina Turner or a Marilyn Monroe, but he scraped the bottom of the fat ugly barrel to get her!" I got out of the car and walked a couple of feet behind him. He didn't turn around to look. When I was about a foot and a half behind him, she and I both stopped walking. I said, "Yeah, Mitch, is this another one of your ho's you fucking," Carolyn responded, "I ain't no Damn ho." I said, "Mitch, she called me and told me to come up here." Carolyn stood there, looking like a monkey. "Yeah, Mitch," she said, "You told me you were separated and getting a divorce. Are you?" Mitch stuttered, "Well, well, we have been separated." I asked Mitch, "Are we separated now?" Mitch did not answer. Carolyn said, "Mitch has been to my house in San Diego and stayed overnight several times, and my girls adore him. We have gone camping together, to the movies, and out to dinner. We did things as if we were a family." She said, "He told me once you guys were divorced, we would get married." Mitch angrily started yelling, "I didn't tell you that, and I've never stayed at your house before!" She asked,

"Why are you lying? I can call my daughters right now, and they will tell you he has." I said, "Let me tell you the same thing I've told his other whore's: the only thing you're going to get from him is a wet black ass." Mitch, if this is what you want when you leave work tomorrow from Arco, you go back to San Diego, where you've been playing house." Mitch said, "Fossy, you shouldn't even be here when I left the house; you were in the bed sleep." I said, "Mitch, I was in bed but, asshole, every shut -eye ain't asleep." I turned and walked away and got back in my car and went home. What was so significant about that day is it was January 4, my youngest son's birthday. Mitch got home early that morning, showered, fixed an alcoholic beverage, changed clothes, and prepared to go somewhere, as he always did. The kids and I got ready to leave. He came over to me and said, "Well, since you found out about her, you can't do shit about it, and where will you go with all these kids? "Ain't shit; you can do." I told Mitch he needed therapy because he was sick and needed mental help. He said, "I ain't the one that's sick, you are" I said, "You're right, I need mental help for staying with your abusive, drunk, whorish Ass all these years!" Later, that evening while the kids and I were home, I called Lina a neighbor to babysit the kids, which she agreed. I went to visit my friend Shellie we talked and had a couple of beers. As we talked, she told me that her husband told her about this woman that Mitch had been dating. I said, "Girl, what else is new?" She asked how I put up with him cheating, I said he's been doing it for so long it blends into our marriage. The Marine Corps seems to be okay with his infidelity and being abusive. Shellie said, "You are a better woman than me because I would kill my husband." I said, "It's not worth it because I would go to jail, then who would take care of my kids?" I left her house around 8:30 p.m. and decided to take a shortcut through the base to get home. I had a hunch. I should go the way that would take me past Mitch's job. When I arrived at his job, all lights were off at his building, but his car was parked at the Motor Pool. I wondered where he could be. I parked and walked around the side of the building and turned one of the doorknobs, thinking Mitch must have duty, but he didn't tell me. I sneaked in while he was on the phone. Mitch talks loud, and I could hear every word that came out of his filthy mouth. He was talking to some female, and he was saying to her how he enjoyed having sex with her, and she must have responded something about oral sex, because his response was, "Your mouth felt good wrapped around it."

Soon after I arrived, another car pulled up, so I went back and walked by my car as if I was getting out of it. The Corporal and I walked in at the same time. He asked was Sergeant Bookman inside. I said, "Yeah, I think so; his car is here." He and I walked in Mitch's office together, and I said, "Hey Mitch, what's going on?" Mitch immediately told the person on the phone that he had to go, and he quickly slammed down the phone. He asked the CPL what he needed as I sat at one of the desks reading. They finished their Military business then the CPL exited the building. I said, "Mitch, you didn't tell me you had duty." He said, "I don't," I asked "Are you waiting for one of your whore's? "Who was the bitch you were on the phone with?" He asked, "When?" He walked up to me and told me I shouldn't have come there, he pushed me against the wall, and I fell to the floor. I got up and brushed the back of my dress off while we were yelling and cussing at each other. I said, "Okay, you Motherfucker, this time, I'm going to kill your fucking ass." I got back in my car and waited a few minutes; he walked to another building. I started the car and put it in drive and tried to run his Ass over. As I drove toward him, he ran to the car's side and yelled, "Are you crazy? You're going to kill me!" I said, "Mitch, I'm so tired of you hitting me, listening to all your lies, and putting up with your whore's" I chased him to another building, which he ran inside. I waited a few minutes for Mitch to come out when he didn't; I went home. While driving home, crying, and asking myself, "What are you doing? Why are you allowing this man to keep abusing you?" I guess the splattered hot oil on his chest wasn't a wake-up call for him. I don't know what to do or where to go!" As I cried, I said, "Lord, what can I do, this is not going to stop, and the Marine Corps won't help me.

"Please stop! I don't feel like being beaten today"...

Was I implying that he could beat me tomorrow?

Chapter 11
NO MORE TEARS TO CRY

My husband was a male whore! I knew for sure when Mitch left the house, if he wasn't going to work, to the Commissary, or the package store (sold alcohol), he was probably in some woman's bed. Mitch and another Marine named Winston had met and started hanging out together. Mitch knew I hated this guy. Winston wasn't married, so he always had girls and Mitch over to his apartment. I knew if Mitch and Winston were socializing they were getting drunk, at a club or at his or some woman's apartment.

One warm day Rona (married) but not to a

Marine and I were sitting on her front porch in Oceanside. We were talking about kids, spouses and stuff. I told her I was married to a Marine and that he was an alcoholic and abusive. She said, "Yeah, I sort of knew that he was abusing you." I asked, "What made you think that?" She enlightened me when Mitch and other Marines were at Winston's home getting drunk, they would always talk about how they controlled their wives with a slap. "I thought Wow, poor women, how these Marines carried on about them." I told Rona on certain evenings Mitch would have some of his drunken Marine buddies over to the house. One particular evening, I was in the kitchen cleaning, and I overheard them talking about us-their wives. Mitch said, "I have to slap Fossy around a bit to make her obey, and the guys laughed. He continued, 'Women are like rugs, you have to beat them every once in a while to keep them in shape." Rona didn't know that Mitch and I were married but separated. She told me that Mitch had been messing around with one of the girls who worked at the hospital with her. She only knew her first name: Donna. When Mitch had cook-outs at our house, a girl name Donna would come over with Winston and a couple of other girls, I didn't think anything because I stayed in my bedroom most of the evening. The rumors about Mitch and Donna seemed to be the talk of the town, so I had to find out who she was. I eventually found out that the rumors were true. Donna and Mitch were dating, she was married to a Marine as well – they had two children. Rona told me Mitch would bring Donna lunch three to four times a week during her break, and she asked, "Fossy, why don't you come by?" I said, "Nope, been there done that." One evening while the kids were sleeping, I drove over to Winston's and knocked on his door. He answered with a dumb look on his face. I asked if Mitch was there, and he said he would get him for me. He shut the door in my face, I pushed the door opened Mitch, was sitting on the couch with some females. I asked Mitch, "What in the hell are you doing here with these ho's?" He replied, "It's not what you think." "Then what the hell is it?" Winston said, "Fossy, you have to leave because I don't want any problems in my house." I replied, "You no-good Motherfucker, you know he is married, and you continue to set him up with these ho's." I walked out, slamming the door, and walked to where Winston and Mitch's cars were parked. I found the most massive brick that I could carry and busted Mitch's and Winston's front windshields. I went home and started packing the rest of his clothes and stacked them in the garage.

Mitch came home early morning, about 2:00 a.m. I was lying in bed but was not asleep. As I was lying there, Mitch said to me, "You know I had to pay for Winston's windshield." I said, "Good! Cause he's paying for your whores, so now you're even." Mitch took his boxes from the garage and loaded them in his car, and left for a few days. I didn't call him, and he didn't call me. Saturday, the boys had baseball practice; I packed their gear and took them to practice since Mitch wasn't home to take them. When I pulled up, Donna was sitting in his car. Mitch had already walked to the baseball field, so I took the boys over to where he was. Then, I walked around the back of the car over to her side, which scared her. I asked, "What the fuck are you doing in my husband's car?" She answered, "We were bringing my boys to practice." I said, "So you are

Donna, and you had the audacity to come to my house with Winston while you were fucking Mitch." She said, "Mitch told me you were divorced!" "We are separated but not legally." "I said, "He is a liar!" I opened the car door, pulled that bitch out by her hair, and start beating the shit out of her. She started yelling for Mitch; evidently, he didn't hear her because he didn't come to her rescue. After I beat her to a pulp, she started running from the direction of the car, but she didn't leave. I walked over to where Mitch was so no one could hear me, I said, "That bitch you had in your car, "I just beat the shit out of her." Other parents were looking as Mitch, and I walked back to the street, and a big argument transpired. Donna was crying and yelling, "You told me you and your wife are divorced!" I asked Mitch, "Does her husband know you are fucking her?" Donna interjected, "We are separated," I told Mitch, "I am going to call your command to let them know you are fucking another Marine's wife." He said I could do what I wanted. I walked back to the baseball field and waited for practice to end. The boys asked if dad was coming home with us, I said, "No, he was going home with someone else." After the confrontation with Donna I was embarrassed and angry. I allowed the abuse that I endured with Mitch take me out of my character. I was angry with myself, which led to my lashing out against Donna. I was infuriated with the Marine Corps for not protecting me from my abusive husband, I was enraged with Mitch for beating me for so many years, and I was disappointed with myself for allowing the abuse. Mitch and Donna's husband Donald knew each other from around the base, at different clubs, and our kid's sports events, but they were not hanging-out friends. Later, that week I was on the base shopping, and saw Donald. We walked toward each other it was such an awkward situation for me. I said hello, and asked how he was doing. He said, "Not too good." I continued, "Well, I guess you know my husband, Mitch, is living with your wife." He said, "Yeah, I found out when I went home one day, and he was sitting on my couch. I asked, 'What's going on, man?' Mitch said, "Checking if your boys will be at practice." I didn't think much about it until later I asked one of my boys did this man constantly come over to the house? My oldest son said 'Yeah, Dad, sometimes he sleeps over with Mom.' I told Donald, I called Mitch's Staff Sergeant and informed him that he was living with another Marine's wife, and the only thing he said was, "Mrs. Bookman, I will talk with him when I see him." Whether the Staff Sergeant spoke with him about it, I don't know but,

Mitch continued to live with her." Mitch came home after several days and acted as if nothing had happened. He had a large box of chocolate candy, and I'm sorry written on the front of the envelope." I didn't open to read the lies on the inside. Later that week, there was a Change of Command and a party that Mitch attended. He came home drunk at 1900/7:00 p.m. on this particular evening. As soon as he walked in, he went to the bedroom to change his uniform. A few minutes later, he came into the kitchen where I was cooking and gulping on some strong Rum & coke instead of beer. I had self-promoted to Liquor for my coping mechanism, to put up with Mitch's shit and be numb when the beatings started. He looked into the skillet on the stove, and asked what I was cooking for dinner. I answered, "Tacos and burritos." He said, "I don't want that shit," he slapped me across my face so hard from the thrust of it I fell into the refrigerator then to the floor. I laid there for a moment then pushed myself up to get off the floor. I stared at Mitch with so much hatred in my eyes but not one teardrop fell. Mitch sat and started watching TV. Mitch threatened that I should cook something else, or he would beat the shit out of me. Even though my jaw was hurting, I removed chicken from the freezer, soaked it in cold water, and cleaned up the mess from the meat on the floor. I went to the bathroom to check if I had a bruise on my face which I did. After 30 minutes, he asked if the food was ready. I explained that I had to defrost the chicken. He told me to hurry because he was hungry. He went to fix himself another Rum & coke. Dinner was ready, he and the kids ate, and I proceeded to clean up the kitchen. By the time I got the kids ready for bed, Mitch was drunk, and I was tipsy. I was in the living room watching TV when he came looking for me. I said "I'm going to bed" he said, "Good because that's where I want you." I said, "Mitch, please not tonight. I am not in the mood for sex, and I don't feel like getting beat up." He shrugged his shoulders and said, "Too bad." I was in a state of no return that night; I felt very numb and scared. As we went into the bedroom, I went to the bathroom to bathe which I was not in a hurry. Mitch was lying on the bed, and I was praying for him to fall asleep. He yelled and asked what was taking me so long. When I went into the bedroom, he held up two of his Khaki uniform belts and a pair of my pantyhose. I closed my eyes and lay on the bed, not knowing what would happen. I begged him, please don't abuse me anymore. He said, "No, I'm not; I'm just going to tie you up, then fuck you all night." What could I do? He made me lay on my back and tied my hands to the bedpost with the pantyhose, then tied each foot with a belt to the bottom bedpost. Mitch laid his drunk, heavy, smelly body on me. He started biting on my nipples then performing oral sex. The touch of his wet tongue made me sick. After the oral sex, he got up and walked to the side of the bed for fellatio. He said, "You know what's going to happen if you bite me, I will kill you." After the disgusting unwanted sexual act, Mitch went into the bathroom to pee, came out, got in the bed on his knees, and started spitting all over my body while rubbing it over me. As I lay there tied up, he inserted his penis in my vagina very abruptly. He was so drunk and tired that all he could do was lie there. He started biting me on my abdomen and torso area then, he rolled over and lay still on the bed but not sleep. As I lay there silently for twenty minutes, he got up and attempted to flip me on my stomach, but the belts prevented me from rolling over. He untied both hands from the pantyhose and one leg from a belt. He forced me on my knees, and he inserted his penis in my vagina from the back. He said, "This isn't working." Mitch's penis would not erect. He went into the kitchen, brought back a long hard object, leaned on the bed, and jabbed it straight up my Ass. I yelled out loudly, but no one could hear my screams. As much as it hurt, I did not cry. Mitch was chanting and groaning some erotic sounds, as I yelled, "Mitch, please stop!" Mitch pulled it out after three minutes. After that traumatic experience, I felt fatigued, embarrassed, ashamed, and sore. I had "No more tears to cry." He finally just lay on the bed and went to sleep. I was able to untie myself, and went and soaked in the bathtub while feeling so numb and degraded. I went to check on the kids later. They were still sleeping. When I came back into the room, I peeked in on Mitch, he was snoring. I had thoughts of killing him again.

Abuse is Not a One Size Fit All.

Chapter 12
War Room
[Warning Graphic Content]

One fall morning, I woke up and decided: no more beatings! I knew Mitch was going TAD (Temporary Additional Duty) somewhere. I didn't care where just as long as I could make my escape. In my thinking scheme, I knew this was the perfect time for me to escape with the kids. For days, I had driven around Oceanside, California, looking for an apartment. After three or four days of searching, I located an apartment, put a deposit down, and signed a lease for our move-in-date. I set up our move with a local moving company. I had set up a separate credit union account, and had money stashed away in the garage where I hid my gun. Shortly after Mitch went TAD, so I started packing clothes, furniture, and other items that we needed. I left him with his clothes, uniforms, and some furniture, including the vile bed that I had so many horrifying, painful, traumatic experiences. The moving company showed up the next day. I was relieved to get away from that monster! After I had been in my apartment for nearly a month, psychologically, I was still restricted. During the late evenings, I suffered from the psychological and emotional pain of mortifying thoughts and nightmares that intangibly shackled my memories. However, I went on with my life, met new friends, and felt free and relieved that I had not been raped, tortured, or beaten for days. A few weeks later, I began hearing talk around the community that Mitch was home, and he was looking for us. I was so frightened that he would find us that I kept the boys out of school for a few days. A few weeks past and I had a sigh of relief since he had not found us yet, and our lives were back to normal at least that's what I thought. On a Tuesday morning, as the boys were getting ready for school, there was a knock at the door, I thought it was one of the neighbor kids that normally come over to ride or walk to school with my boys. As I opened the door, Mitch was standing in front of me, my heart channeled to my stomach then to my feet. I did not invite him in, but Mitch pushed past me as I tried to push him out. As we struggled, I hit him in the head a few times, but he just shoved past me and walked in. He asked, "What in the fuck do you think you're doing?" I said, "Mitch, I can't go through any more of your abuse."

He asked where the boys were, and I told him they were in their room getting dressed. By that time, the boys heard his voice and ran out the bedroom shouting, "Daddy, Daddy!" He hugged each one of them. I told Mitch he had to leave since I had to walk the boys to the bus stop. He said he would wait here until I got back. After I returned to the apartment, I searched for my purse and keys, so I could run out the front door to get away from this Bastard! I grabbed my keys and told Mitch I had an appointment I had to get to by 10:00 a.m. He said, "Call them and cancel it because you ain't going no fucking where." My life flashed in front of my face because I didn't know if I would leave in an ambulance, a body bag, or my kids find me dead when they came home. I knew he wasn't going to allow me to leave, so I went to clean the kitchen. Mitch was sitting at the kitchen table. He had taken off his Cammie jacket. He then raised his voice and said, "You need to pack up the kids and come back home, or I will move in here with you guys." I said, "No, we are not moving back with you, and you can't move in with us because you are not on the lease." Why did I say that? The next thing I knew, he grabbed my hair, pushed me up against the sink, and started kissing me. He pulled me to the bedroom and threw me towards the wall. This time I knew that I might not win this War, but this Battle I was about to fight was for my life and for my kids to have a Mother. When he started unbuttoning his trousers to remove them, he bent forward to untie his military boots. I grabbed his head while trying to poke out his eyes. He lifted his head then hit me with his right arm across my stomach to push me away. I started beating him on his back, he pushed me up against the dresser, and I started hitting him with all the strength in my body. I had ironed the kid's clothes that morning, so the ironing board was still standing upright with the iron sitting on the ironing board's narrow end, and the cord wrapped around it. The next thing I knew, Mitch slung me on the bed and said, "Get your Ass, undressed." I was begging with Mitch, "Please, no more!" I jumped off the bed, and he grabbed me and threw me on the bed again. I grabbed his arm to bite it, and somehow he managed to pull his arm from my teeth. He was bleeding. I was kicking and punching him as all the adrenaline circulated rapidly through my body. Mitch wasn't a small man. I hit him again he then struck me across the right side of my face I knew I had to give up. I was sore and so exhausted, but he didn't seem to be. Mitch knew I had never fought him this way before. Fighting him got him angry. While gritting his teeth, he mumbled, "You are my wife, and I can do with you what I want."

Then, the torture began. Mitch had been drinking. I could smell alcohol on his breath. He pushed me back on the bed, he got on top of me as I was punching him on his sides and back to get him off me. He slapped me and said "turn your Ass over." I wrestled with him because I knew what was going to happen. Somehow he flipped me over, and I fell on the floor. He grabbed the iron off the ironing board. I was sitting on the floor with my back up against the bed as he grabbed the iron. He held the iron over my head and said, "Suck my dick!" "I will jab you in the top of your head if you bite me" I was crying no, no for him to stop. He repeated, "If you don't want to die today do what I said Bitch!" I clenched my fist as I wanted to bite him with all my teeth and strength. Mitch acted as if he was demented. I knew if I had bitten him, he would have killed me. After about five minutes of agony, the real, sodomizing began. After he gratified himself from my sore and achy mouth, he stepped back and exited the room. I thought he was going to clean himself up and leave for work. Slowly and painfully I lay across my bed while thinking, "Oh, thank you, Jesus, this man is leaving," only to have him return with my broom. I took a painful, hard sigh as I lay across the bed, scared and naked. He instructed, "Turnover on your back." I was crying and screaming, "Mitch, please don't!" It seemed as though the louder I cried, the more it turned him on. That Maniac, Marine Monster, with a hard jab and twist, inserted that broom in my vagina and sodomized me with it for about ten minutes as he was massaging his penis while trying to get it erected. He stopped to pull the broom out of my vagina and tried to turn me on my stomach. I punched him in his face. He said, "Oh, now you want to fight again?" That man punched me so hard that I thought he knocked some of my teeth from my mouth. As Mitch got me on my stomach, he grabbed the iron again and told me to get on my "fucking knees." All this torture is happening while I am crying and praying so profusely. I knew I was going to die that morning. He asked "Where was the Vaseline?" I said, "I don't have any," He said, "You better find me something, or I will force this broom, up your Ass without anything on it." I told Mitch I only had Crisco Oil (solid) he went into the kitchen to lubricate the broom handle. I was screaming and crying so loud, but no one heard me. Mitch returned and forced me on my knees. He lubricated the broom handle and stuck it in my rectum/Ass while sliding it in and out. It felt as though he was twisting it as well. I was screaming in agony, but there was nothing I could do. Mitch asked as he shoved that broom handle harder, "Are you coming back home?" I said, "Yes," in a harrowing and somber tone as I gripped the sheet on the bed. Mitch finally stopped torturing me with that broom handle after about 15 minutes. Mitch finally pulled that broom from my rectum/Ass, I was bleeding and in so much agonizing pain that I couldn't move. As he finished, he got up, walked over to my dresser, took out pantyhose, and tied me to the bed. He said, "I'm tired and want to take a nap, and I want to make sure you don't get away." I said, "Mitch, I need to go to the bathroom because I'm bleeding." He responded, "Suffer." I pleaded with him again, so he let me go to the bathroom while threatening I had better not try to call anyone or runaway. As soon as I got into the bathroom, I looked in the mirror. I had a large bruise on the right side of my face and my right arm. I put cold water on my face. I sat down to use the bathroom, which my entire body throbbed. Blood was dripping slowly from my vagina and rectum I did not know which way to wipe as I was in excruciating pain. I stayed in the bathroom for at least fifteen minutes. He had not let me close the door. I heard him snoring. Mitch always fell asleep quickly, especially if he had been drinking or after sex. When I went back to the bed, he woke up quickly, and he tied my hands to the bedposts then he went back to sleep. I lay beside him in so much pain and asking God, "Why, why have you forsaken me?" It was a few minutes after 11:00 a.m. when I glanced at the clock on the nightstand. After thirty minutes, Mitch woke up and went into the kitchen to drink and eat as I lay there, in affliction. After he finished eating, he said, "Well, I feel like fucking you again." I was tied up and in pain, and there was nothing I could do. He went into the boy's room and came back with a belt, and I turned my head and closed my eyes, wondering, "What is he going to do? He came over and untied me and told me to lean across the bed. I said, "Mitch, why do you keep doing this to me? You know I am in so much pain." He said, "I don't care; you shouldn't have tried to leave me." Mitch went into the bathroom to wet one of the belts, came back into the bedroom, hit me continually across my Ass, then licked it and said, "I want to make it feel better." Then another hit, then another – he did this several times, then he stopped for about five minutes, as I lay there silently because I had no more to moan or no more groans. When Mitch finished beating me with the belt, he turned me over and said, "Now I will make love to you." As if this man would know how to do that! He started licking all over my body which I wanted to vomit. He turned me over and gave one long lick with his tongue across my Ass and said, "This bruise on your Ass means you are branded for life with me bitch, you belong to me!" Well, I'm not going to bruise you too bad because you still have to take care of the kids. Your Ass will be sore for a while, and this torment will make you bring your Ass back home because if not, I will come over here every day until you do." Sobbing, I explained that I had to give a thirty-day notice to the apartment complex. He said as he was getting dressed; for me to get myself and the kids some clothes for now, and we would start moving my "damn furniture" over the weekend. Before he walked out the door, he told me to clean myself up because the kids would be home soon. As he walked towards the door, he stopped and said, "Don't go to my command." As soon as Mitch left, I painfully walked into the bathroom. I looked in the mirror, I had bruises across my face, arms, legs, Ass, and about every inch of my body, what could I do, where could I go? I took a long, hot shower and bath as I tried to wash my skin off my body. I was in so much pain. I scrubbed and scrubbed to get his scent and the smell of rape and liquor off my body. I had two hours before the boys came home. I got in my car and headed to the base to see a doctor. But, these thoughts appeared in my mind: the kids; no money; security blanket; where could I go; the Marine Corps won't help. About three miles from the base hospital, I turned around. Crying and praying what I should do – what could I do – I went back to my apartment. While sitting on my bed crying, and thinking about the torture, the shame, the humiliation, and sexual abuse, I blamed God because he could have changed the error of Mitch's abusive behavior. Instead, God allowed Mitch to torture me year after year. In my heart, I believed God had forsaken me. This man was my husband for better or worse. I never thought the Battle that I had to fight would be against him. #IGOTOUT!

Is there a radiation treatment to ease the memories of emotional and psychological trauma caused by Physical Abuse?

Chapter 13
REAL LIVES OF FORMER MARINE WIVES (These are their stories)

FREDA

As I mentioned earlier, Freda was married to Hennison. Freda had a daughter named Tasha, who was Hennison's step-daughter, and he hated Tasha. Freda's house was always filthy, she did not work, and she was lazy as hell, but she loved going to play bingo. Hennison was a cruel callus son-of-a-bitch Marine and he had no respect for his wife or women. Hennison's beliefs about women were they get pregnant, clean the house, cook, and open their legs for their husbands or partners whenever they wanted sex. Hennison said belittling, cruel, and hurtful words to Freda during the times we were cooking out, playing cards, dominoes, or just socializing.

Freda was a great card player, and Hennison was envious of her playing card ability. He and Freda would fight when they came to visit. Sometimes Hennison would get angry if Freda beat him in cards or if they were partners, and they lost to Mitch and I. Hennison would become angry and lean across the table and slap her in the face. Depending on how he felt, he would lean forward to punch her in the breast; she had big breasts. Freda would occasionally throw her drink in his face, and when she did, Hennison would grab her hair and sling her from the chair to the floor.

Hennison would make Freda sit on the floor and dare her to move, saying, "If you move, I will kick the shit out of you." One of his all-time hateful remarks he often told Freda was if she didn't act like a wife, he would "launch her fat Ass." As I watched Freda get beat by her Maniac Marine husband, I could not say or do anything because Mitch would slap or punch me for interfering. I'd ask myself, which was worse, physical abuse or emotional and psychological abuse? Mitch was physically abusive to me which hurt in a different way. Hennison was verbally abusive to the point that his wife and step-daughter shivered in tears, from the cruel and defaming words he would say to them. He would call them: stupid, fat, ugly, or stinky and tell Freda, "Other men don't want you, you're only good for fucking, and sometimes you don't do that right; I should launch your fat ugly ass for a younger wife."

One day I was at Freda's to just chat and drink beer. We sat in the living room until Hennison came home. He said, "Hi Foxy," – he always called me Foxy and not Fossy. He looked at Freda and asked, "What did your fat Ass cook today?" then asked, "Where is your fat-Ass ugly daughter?" By that time, the front door had shut behind me, but I could still hear them arguing as I walked down the stairs.

The next day Freda came to the house; she had a black eye. She explained, "That Motherfucker snatched me off the couch, pulled my hair, threw me into the kitchen, and told me that I better cook him something to eat before he put my ugly-Ass daughter and me out. When I refused, he punched me in the eye." I asked if she cooked him something to eat, she said, "Hell, No." We started laughing at the moment. I told her I was fearful of Mitch coming home because I know it's going to be some shit with him, but I put up with his shit for my babies. She said, "Well, I don't have any babies with this Motherfucker, and I'm sick and tired of his abuse." Freda and Tasha would come to the house to eat. Freda told me Hennison would not buy food to cook because she wouldn't cook the meals that he wanted to eat. He said, "Tasha ain't my daughter, so I don't care if the two of you starve to death." Several times I gave Freda money for the Commissary or food to eat.

I went to visit Freda one evening since I had not heard from her or didn't see her drive or walk past our house. She told me, "Girl, I tried to kill that bastard last night." Tasha had gone into the kitchen to get something to eat, and Hennison told her not to go in his refrigerator. Freda said she got up and went in the kitchen to feed her, Hennison came in and pushed Tasha and said, "Didn't I tell your fat-

Ass you can't have anything to eat. You are too fat and sloppy as it is?"

Freda said "Fossy, before I knew it, I grabbed the giant pot that was sitting on the stove and start hitting him on his side and back, he grabbed me, and we fell to the floor. He got on top of me and started punching me in my face like I was a man, Tasha started crying and was beating on his back and saying, "get off my mom!" The next thing I knew, he took his fist and pushed Tasha with so much force that she flew up against the cabinets. Then I lost it. The adrenaline circulated through my body, and somehow I was able to get from under that asshole, and I jumped up. While he was still on the floor, I kicked him in his face, back, and wherever my size ten shoes could kick him. Tasha grabbed the broom and started hitting him as well. He then curled in a fetal position and yelled, 'I'm going to kill you Assholes when I get off this floor if you are still in my house. I told Tasha to run to Ms. Fossy's house. When he got up, I ran to the bedroom and grabbed my gun, and threatened him, 'Motherfucker, if you come near me again, the Military Police will be taking you out in a Marine Corps body bag." Freda separated from Hennison, they divorced.

SANA

Sana was married to Omar (Marine), she was known as the Jezebel babysitter whore of base housing. Sana was pretty with a medium build. She was in her late thirties, we the other Marine wives were in our early twenties. Sana had three kids when she married Omar, which each of her children had three different daddy"s. Sana never discussed any physical abuse between them, but we heard the verbal abuse. Omar always referred to Sana as his whore or his lazy bitch. Marines enjoyed visiting Omar; they knew if they went to pee, Sana would come in and give them a blow job. Sana was known around the base and neighborhood as giving awesome blow jobs and loved having anal sex. Omar was aware of his wife's reputation and knew some Marines that she had sex with or fellatio. Sana and my sister Polly had become good friends.

Mitch and I were looking for a babysitter for our youngest son. Polly told us that Sana provided childcare for Marine families. One day I went to her house to ask her about watching our son, which she said she could. When I started taking my son to Sana, she fell in love with him. Some mornings I would drop him off and other mornings Mitch would. Rumors were that Sana would have sex with the

Marine dads when they dropped off their kids. Some mornings, I would suggest to Mitch that I would take our son to Sana; often times, he said, "Oh, that's okay, I will take him." Even though I had suspicions but wasn't sure that he and Sana were having sex, but seeing is believing.

After Mitch went to drop off our son one morning, I waited for five minutes and drove a different way to get to her house. When I pulled up, Mitch was already inside, and Omar had already gone to work. Sana always left her back door unlocked for her kids. On this particular morning, Sana took our son and laid him on the sofa instead of the bed. As I listened through the door opening, Sana asked Mitch, "Do you want head or want it in my Ass?" Mitch's response was, "No, I don't have time, so just suck it for a minute." She said,

"Motherfucker, you better not come in my mouth like you did yesterday." He said, "Just suck it bitch."

As Mitch was pulling up his Cammie pants, I slipped out the door that I came in. I didn't know rather to poison him when he got home or pack my kids to leave, but I did neither. When you are a battered spouse, there are a couple of things you learn to do: be "Shut Mouth Grace" and "Choose Your Battles." At least I knew these were the best choices for me. When Mitch came home that evening, he smelled like a drunk. He asked me to make dinner, but I refused because I was angry and upset. Mitch pushed me and I fell on the sofa, he leaned down towards me and slapped me so hard across my face. Mitch said, "Why do you make me do these things to you?" I went into the bathroom to look at my face, and I had a long black and blue mark. I chose not to say anything about him and

Sana's sexual affair. In September 2018, Polly decided to tell me that Sana and Mitch had sex with each other when she babysat our son, I told her, "I already knew."

RHONDA

Rhonda and Mick were another married couple we would socialize with at El Toro Marine Corps Air Station. They had three beautiful girls and later a son. Rhonda and Mick were the Marine couple that looked as though they had no marital problems, and other Marine families wanted to imitate. They lived in base housing around the corner from us. When you walked into their home, it was always clean and designed as if it came out of a Home and Gardens Magazine. Our kids went to school together, and we would go to each other's homes for cook-outs and or play cards. Mitch and Mick didn't hang out much together because they didn't want the other to know about their extramarital affairs. I have seen Mick with different women. However, I could not tell Rhonda in fear that if it got back to Mitch, it meant a beat-down for me. Remember, I had to choose my battles.

Rhonda: When I found out Mick was cheating on me, I never reported this behavior to his command. I thought maybe he would stop and realize what he had at home. Mick would abuse me emotionally. Even though there was no hateful name-calling, he would say that he loved me, but he could not stand me or despise me. I never caught him with other women; I possess pictures of lots of women with whom he was cheating. Drea was his favorite mistress. I never received calls from other women, but the children would tell me about female calls for their dad when they answered the phone (landline). Mick would take my girls to his girlfriend's homes to get their hair braided, which my girls would tell me when they came home. When Mick would go shopping, he bought identical negligées for me and whichever girlfriend he was sleeping with at that time. I have pictures to prove it. I have pictures of Drea wearing lingerie that matches what Mick bought for me.

I was at the PX (Base Exchange) with Mick one day, and I remember he bought some perfume that never made it home. Mick's best friend was Omar, and they were thick as thieves! On numerous occasions Omar would cover for Mick so Mick could be with one of his girlfriends. One time, in particular, they left our home together. Later that evening, I called Sana to ask if Omar was home, he was home but Mick was not there with Omar. Mick always had an excuse, either he was TAD (Temporary Additional Duty), or overnight duty, or had to work to the wee hours of the morning. I always knew when Mick was planning to spend time with a woman he took a specific bag, packed certain clothes to take with him, and stayed two to three days. Mick always used the main excuse: 'I was too drunk to drive home,' but he drove to Drea's. I knew for years that he was having affairs with different women, I was fed up with his infidelity and decided to leave him. My children and I moved to Georgia. Mick and I later divorced, and he married Drea. We were married for almost 20 years, and throughout these years, I experienced psychological and emotional trauma. My Marine husband controlled me, manipulated me, and always told me, "Do not go to my command."

DEIDRA

The Bennisleys were another Marine family with which we became friends. They had a son and a daughter. They were a strange-acting and looking family. Deidra was all of five feet, and her husband Floyd was at least 6'4" and skinny. Floyd was a drunk just like Mitch's other Maniac Marine friends. Deidra and I used to hang out together since we lived on the same street. Some days I would visit, Deidra and her eyeglasses would be broken. She would be cooking or watching TV and trying to hold them up, or she would have tape on them. I would ask, "Did Floyd hit you again?" and she would cry. I told her, "You know this abuse that we are suffering in silence has to stop." I have gone to Mitch's command and they won't do anything." She said, "I know, I went to Floyd's as well." I stayed for another hour then I had to leave because Mitch would be coming home soon, and I had to cook dinner. I also had to pretend that I wanted to have sex with him or get the shit beat out of me. We hugged each other; then, I went home. I didn't see Deidra for about three weeks. One day I was walking our dog, so I stopped over. I asked Deidra how she was doing, she said, "Fossy, these beatings have to stop." Deidra's arm had a hard white cast on it, and in a sling. Deidra told me she said to Floyd if he hit her again, she would leave him.

Later that summer, I did not see Deidra or the kids in the neighborhood, so I asked Mitch, "Did Floyd PCS (Permanent Change of Station) 'because I haven't seen Deidra." He said, "No, I heard she went home." I shook my head and went into the bedroom. I knew she separated from him because she couldn't endure any more abuse from the lethal hands of her Maniac Monster of a Marine husband.

VIVIAN

My experience as a Marine Corps wife was not a pleasant one. I was married to a long-time career Marine that had two other wives before me. We met while living in the same apartment complex and begin to date after a few months of our meeting. We got engaged within six months and married soon after. I was a virgin when I married him. I became pregnant a few months after being married, and there began the roller coaster ride as a Marine's wife. I won't say it was all bad, there were some good times, but the unpleasant times stand out most in my mind during the five-year marriage. From the lows of always told the Marine

Corps didn't issue him a wife at boot camp, to the pain of being the victim of verbal and emotional abuse, it was more than I bargained for in the marriage. The life of a Marine's wife was nothing less than miserable, and the benefits were not comparable to the pain and grief I endured being married to this Maniac Marine. I do not knock the Marine Corps because I believe in the mission and the service, however, the individual I was married to, took military service to a different level which I'm sure was not intended by the Marine Corps or Armed Services.

On our first duty assignment, one year after we were married, we moved overseas. From the moment we landed in Japan, it was lonely and dark, as I was left at the hotel and our one-year-old son, while my husband went off to gamble. We were jet-lagged, unfamiliar with our surroundings, and alone.

Since this was my husband's fourth tour, he was right at home and made sure I knew I was on his turf and would behave and conform to his rules. He would always talk about Filipino women and how he loved them. On almost a daily basis, he would say, 'I could get rid of you if I wanted to.' He always made me feel as though I was as disposable as a used paper towel. He resented me questioning anything he did and became angry and verbally abusive if I tried in any way to hold him accountable to his responsibilities as a husband. The most painful memory of his gambling problem was missing our first ultra-sound appointment and gambling our money for bills away without any care or concern. When confronted about this, it was a massive argument over the need for me to remain silent about his irresponsible behavior. During these episodes, I was constantly reminded that the

Marines didn't issue him a wife, insinuating that I was irrelevant in the situation. I remember one of our arguments escalated to severe verbal abuse, and he threatened to take my ID card and disable the car. It was a well-known fact that overseas, the active-duty sponsor was responsible for the dependents, he knew I was powerless and was forced to conform to his emotional and verbal abuse.

Before base housing came available, we lived out in the town, while on the waiting list. One day after an argument, to prevent me from calling my family, he cut the phone line (landline), took my ID card and disabled the car, so I could not leave until he returned from work that evening. I was desperate; I felt backed into a corner and devastated. I managed to wiggle the wires of the phone to get a dial tone. I called a girlfriend I met at church to pick me up and give me a ride to the nearby Air Force Base. She took me to Legal Services, where I was taken to a women's shelter after telling them my story of what I had been going through with my Marine husband. I stayed there for several days without any contact with my husband, and I knew every day he grew angrier and angrier. At that point, I knew I would need to make plans to leave the duty station and return to my family in the States.

As a Department of Defense employee, I had an advantage because I worked on the Air Force Base. I did go to his superiors at the Marine Base; however, I felt that they were not interested in helping me hold my husband accountable for his actions and sided with him. We were going through counseling from our Pastor, and the advice felt like more of the same excuses for the husband to remain irresponsible and aggressively and emotionally abusive. After three and a half years of turmoil, I had enough and asked my boss to help me get back home. I believe his influence as an Air Force Colonel was the saving grace to help me get the furniture packed and move back with my family in the United States.

After being told that he would keep the furniture and my son, I fought to break free from the psychological abuse and bondage I felt I was under with my husband. He always emphasized that he was the active-duty sponsor, and I was the dependent, and had to do what he said; I was at his mercy. This psychological abuse wore on me so much, and I needed to be free of this darkness, loneliness, and emotional trauma. I know many Marine Corps and Military spouses suffer and endure turmoil, psychological, emotional, and physical abuse from their spouses or intimate partners.

I can only hope that one day each of them will have the courage to stand up for themselves as I did and get out of that abusive relationship. After leaving my husband and going through a very bitter divorce, I pulled the pieces of my life back together, raised my son, and moved on with my life. Even though he was a good father to our son in the past, he signed away his parental rights upon our divorce. I was encouraged by my church members to go to therapy. My Marine husband messed me up so bad emotionally that therapy for me was over eleven years, and I was only married to this Maniac Monster of a Marine for five years. I felt abandoned, broken, and cheated. I didn't believe in divorce; my family didn't believe in divorce. I was emotionally broken and needed to be put back together again.

The Marine Corps Chaplain, or the Marine Corps then, did not protect me when I was infringed. I needed to define what I owned because I always thought that it was my fault. I needed to get rid of the emotional and psychological baggage before I went into another relationship and get on with my life. There is a wonderful life afterward, and I can attest that with determination, lengthy therapy, love, and support from family and friends, you too can make it out. I am thankful to be free, and I hold no ill will towards my ex-husband, Hennison, or the Marine Corps. Freda was the first wife of Hennison's #IGOTOUT.

PAMELA

While working at Camp Pendleton Wire Mountain base housing, I met Pamela, Jonas, her

Marine husband, and their two boys and one daughter as Jonas was checking into base housing. Pamela was a timid looking spouse with an adorable shape and a beautiful smile. The first time I saw her, I knew she was experiencing some type of Abuse with Jonas: physical, sexual, emotional, or psychological. She wore Abuse well as so many other spouses, did for so many years. Pamela looked lonely, timid, and afraid to speak.

Over the weeks, she and I became good friends. We would go to each other's home to visit. We would cook lunch or dinner for each other, drink beer or wine coolers, and were happy that we were away from our stupid, abusive husbands. I did not tell Pamela that Mitch was using me as his punching bag because I was afraid she would tell Jonas, and he would tell Mitch. Our husbands had so much control and manipulation over our lives

171

that if they knew we were hanging out three to four times a week, they would forbid us from seeing each other. Pamela and I began to go out to different venues, but I had to convince her to go; she was afraid of Jonas as I was of Mitch. We would go to the Commissary, the Exchange and base clubs, and have fun dancing while turning our frowns into smiles!

Pamela: "My husband's dilemmas were he lied and cheated. When Jonas was stationed in Arizona, I know he was cheating on me even though I had no proof at that time. He was always gone and sometimes would not come home after work. One day he had to leave again, I said, "Wow, the Marines send you a lot of places," He said, "Yes, and I have duty every week." I knew my husband was having affairs with different women, but I could not prove it. When Jonas came home in the wee hours of the mornings he would shower. Jonas would whisper when he spoke on the phone and women would call our landline. Every weekend I found used and unused condoms in different gym bags. I know this was evidence that he was having sex with other women but I did not want to believe it. I confronted him about the condoms, he grabbed my head between his hands and shook it vigorously and said, "Don't you ever question me about what's in my fucking gym bag or where I'm going or been." Then it was San Diego. He was away from home more than when he was stationed in Arizona. He would disappear for two or three days at a time, but he always blamed it on the Marine Corps. When he came home, I found condoms in his gym bag again. When I asked Jonas about them, he said, "another Marine borrowed my bag, and the condoms belonged to him." I still wondered if he was cheating. I was so naive I believed the condoms belonged to another Marine. What more proof did I need?

Jonas went to Desert Storm for a few months. When they all came home, the spouses with kids went to greet our husbands at the airfield. Fathers, husbands, and sons were getting off the plane and greeting each other with kisses, flowers, and candy. When Jonas exited the plane, he walked away from us and went into a building without a kiss, hug, or hello. He ignored our kids and me. He finally came and got in the car after 30 minutes, we drove home, and he didn't say a word to any of us.

Once we arrived home, the kids went out to play, and Jonas took his bags to our room. He finally asked, "How are you and the kids doing?" I said, "Jonas, what happened at the airfield?" He said, 'Nothing,' I said, 'I know nothing, you just walked past us like you didn't see us." He said, "Don't start with me bitch; I'm tired." Jonas had been home at least two weeks, and we only had sex once. I didn't want sex but to keep him from yelling or getting angry with me; I had sex with him. About three weeks later, his bags were still packed, and I looked inside and found a pair of women panties and a picture. Jonas was watching TV; I walked towards him and asked, 'Whose panties are these?' He said, "Those are your panties," I said, "The hell they are!" Jonas went on the defense and asked, 'Why are you going through my fucking bags?' I asked, "Who was the woman in the picture?" He said it was a 'friend' of his. Jonas said, "I'm not having an affair." We argued for a while; then, I gathered the kids to go to the store. We got into the van, my oldest son sat on the back seat

175

where he found a receipt for flowers. Jonas had sent flowers to someone. The note stated: "I love you." I sat and cried for a few minutes, then drove to the store.

Jonas got stationed in Beaufort, South Carolina. He had the same whorish problems. Different women called my house, and some came to the house looking for him. He would disappear for days at a time. One early Saturday morning, Jonas got home at 2:30. Jonas came into the bedroom, and I asked him where he had been. Jonas smelled as if he just had sex. I asked him which of his whores was he with? We started arguing. He pushed me onto the bed jumped on top of me and started choking me. I was gasping for my breath then he removed his hands from around my neck. I was hysterical and told Jonas to sleep on the couch. Later that same week, my girlfriend Lucy went to visit her family that lived in Beaufort, South Carolina. While she was home, her sister Nita showed her a picture of her and her new boyfriend. In shock, Lucy said, "What! That's my girlfriend's Pamela's husband." Nita said, "No, it couldn't be; he stays overnight with me every weekend. We go dancing and have cook-outs at the house. Lucy said his name is Jonas. Nita said, "No, his name is Lame." Lucy tried to convince Nita that the man she was dating was Jonas, but she did not believe her. When Lucy came home, she gave me the photo I later showed it to Jonas, and of course, he denied that he was dating her. I asked Jonas where the picture was taken, and who was the woman? Jonas said she was a Marine, and they were at an event. As I turned to walk away, he grabbed me by my hair and said "Bitch didn't I tell you not to question me?"

While married to Jonas, I found women's hygiene products, panties, bras, earrings, and love notes, which I knew these items did not belong to me or were not for me. I knew Jonas was having numerous affairs; I still went with him to each of his duty stations. Did the cheating stop? No. He was my love; he was my husband; he was the father of my children. I had limited education, he was my security blanket. I was not a happy Marine wife because Jonas cheated on me for the twenty-five years that we were married, which consisted of his seven duty stations. I hated the Marine Corps because I thought they kept my husband away from my kids and me. He would always tell me that the Marine Corps would send him to school, TAD, or he had duty. But, little did I know he was having affairs with different women at every duty station, and other Marines would cover for him. I guess that's what the Marines meant by 'Band of Brothers.'

Jonas never hit me with a closed fist or open hands he would grab my head between his two hands while shaking my head aggressively, or choke me. He would always say in anger, 'Do not go to my command! Do not fuck up my career!' I sustained a tremendous amount of Emotional Abuse, Psychological Abuse, and excessive cheating from my Marine husband. I finally divorced Jonas; then, he married one of his mistresses. In the 70s and 80s, the support was not available for the Marine Corps wives and most of us were alone and felt abandoned. My advice to each of you: if you are married to military personnel or have an intimate military partner, and you are being abused (physically, emotionally, or sexually), please go to their Command, Family Advocacy, or the Chaplain.

Civilians, please call your local Domestic Violence Hotline or 911. Please make someone listen! The only people that listened to me were other Marine wives experiencing the same type of Abuse. I could not go to Jonas' command because he threatened me, controlled me, and manipulated me. I love my children more than anything on this earth, but I regretted marrying Jonas. Spouses don't ignore the signs of your significant other cheating. I told family and friends that Jonas never abused me while we were married but he did. He squeezed my head between his hands and choked me. I thought since he didn't hit me with open hands or closed fists then it wasn't abuse but it was!

Don't wear the War Paint to cover up the Battle scars from physical Abuse. You are a different generation of Military spouses and or

Intimate Partners; you have unlimited resources utilize them or please #GETOUTNOW!

If someone tells you they are being abused,

please don't ask "why do you stay?"

If you have never been in an

abusive relationship

you will never know or understand

why we stay!

Chapter 14
THE MARINES
PROTECTED OUR COUNTRY,
BUT WHO PROTECTED US?

After all the beatings, after all the body kicks, after all the bruises, after all the rape episodes and being sodomized by my Marine husband, I found my grain of courage and ounce of strength to divorce Mitch in 1998. When I informed my attorney that I wanted a divorce based on abuse and infidelity she said "In the State of California, the laws only recognize Irreconcilable Differences. Funny, the State didn't recognize a wife getting the shit beat out of her from her husband! "I lived as a Marine Wife and experienced a Battered Life for many years. I learned to live with my pain, shame, guilt, and humiliation, in silence, which led to having NO SELF WORTH, NO SELF ESTEEM, & NO IDENTITY.

Congress established the Transitional Compensation Benefits Program as an entitlement for abused dependents of military personnel in the Fiscal Year 1994 Department of Defense (DOD) Authorization Act (P.L. 103-160). Should the Marine Corps and the Armed Forces compensate the battered wives during this era under this Program? "Yes." Should there be a statute of limitations for prosecution for the abuser and its tenant or component? "No." "While these Marines Protected Our Country Who Protected Us?" As stated previously, we didn't have the effective

Family Advocacy Programs or the Department of Defense Domestic Abuse Task Force.

As a woman, Mother, and wife, I lived through some of the most painful Abuse that any person should ever have to experience, I survived for my kids.

Abuse hid its face from our children; Abuse hid its face from our family; Abuse hid its face in one of the most respected Military uniforms in the world, the United States Marine Corps. Abuse does not discriminate amongst age, race, gender, or social economics. Abuse doesn't care whether your spouse or intimate partner wears a uniform or a suit to work, wears pants, or a dress has a military rank or has a title. Abuse is vicious, and it will deprive you of your dignity, self-esteem, and self-worth.

I didn't finish high school because I was pregnant, so I dropped out of school. I was a confused, teenage mother and wife. In 1978, I obtained a GED while still being brutally beat, tortured, and sexually assaulted. Mitch was jealous of me while I was a student – sometimes he would throw my books in the trash – I never gave up on pursuing my education. I eventually finished my GED only to pursue a Ph.D.

There are still episodes of Abuse that I didn't include in my story; some were as graphic as those you've read. When Mitch asked me to marry him, I was 16, naive, immature, and I loved him. ABUSE Concealed its face in our marriage vows, but Abuse Revealed its face inside the liquor that Mitch Consumed. Please #GETOUTNOW!

Women are like 'RUGS, you have to beat them

every once in a while to keep them in shape."

- Unknown-

Chapter 15
TRAUMATIC TRIGGERS

TRAUMA

"Trauma is when we have encountered an out of control, frightening experience that has disconnected us from all sense of resourcefulness or safety or coping or love." (Brach, 2011)

As an abused woman, wife, and Mother, I lived with my pain, silent shame, guilt, and humiliation. Mitch took my "SELF WORTH." After one of Mitch's beatings, he would bring me roses or candy.

WHAT IS A TRIGGER?

A trigger evokes an inevitable reaction from someone when they emotionally or physically reactivate something in their lives. It sends them back to the time they experienced the trauma and causes them to feel distress. For domestic violence survivors, this may mean they begin to evade people, places, and things that awaken the thoughts of the abuser (Rockefeller, 2018).

Mitch thought giving me roses and candy would make me feel better but little did he know they were traumatic triggers for me. Sometimes he stood in front of me crying as tears flowed down his face saying, "I'm sorry." "Sorry, he was." He assumed these "Trauma Triggers "would ease the physical and psychological pain that he subjected me to for so many years. A medical doctor and a psychiatrist can prescribe a pill for physical pain, depression, and mental illness to make his or her patient feel better. Is there a pill I can swallow to dissolve the memories of the emotional and psychological pain of physical abuse?

My disfigurement from physical abuse were: black eyes, broken arms, bruised ribs, sore Ass, scraped knees, busted lips, etc. The physical wounds have healed. The intangible emotional and psychological memories of years of Abuse still haunt my Lower Self.

HOW TRIGGERS AFFECT DOMESTIC VIOLENCE SURVIVORS

Triggers are a significant concern because when something sets off a survivor's memory, the consequences can cause enervating effects. It can compress the survivor emotionally, mentally, and even physically. It's a profound reaction that can influence the exact level of intensity as the initial traumatic occurrence (Rockefeller, 2018).

THE SOURCE OF MY TRAUMATIC TRIGGERS

Red Roses – Roses are beautiful. After a good beating, as Mitch would say, he would buy me a dozen and weep how sorry he was. I referred to them as Roses of Repentance. I don't buy roses because they remind me of past dreadful memories.

Box of Chocolate Candy – You never knew what you would get. I knew. He smashed chocolate pieces down my throat if I didn't have sex with him!

Blue Sequined Gown – Maniac Mitch cut it in pieces. Wearing that gown made me feel like

Cinderella at the Ball. Looking at a Blue Sequined Gown causes me anxiety.

Attics – For decades, I have asked God, "Will you build me a house without an Attic of Thorns? Rape, Torture, Sexual Assault, and Physical Abuse.

Pantyhose – It took years before I could wear pantyhose again. I had flashbacks of my wrists or feet tied while being beat.

Iron – I bought/buy everything "wash and wear, or dry clean only" The thought of the narrow part of my iron jabbed at the cranial part of my head gave me traumatic nightmares for years.

Bedroom Door Locked – Most of my beatings took place in my bedroom behind locked doors. It's a control phobia. Before going to sleep I would check my bedroom lock up to 10 times. In my mind, I was locking out my abuser!

Broom Handle – This is about me being honest to my Readers. The Broom Handle Torture was just that TORTURE. I did not use or buy a broom for at least 15 years. I avoided all grocery aisles with brooms. My Battle was painful in that War Room but # IGOTOUT.

War Paint – No make-up for me; it's a reminder for covering up bruises, scars on my face, arms, legs, and body. I rarely wear War Paint-My Battered Battle is Over!

DRESS BLUES/BRUISE TRIGGERS

When Mitch wore his Dress Blues, he took the slogan "The Few, The Proud, The Marines" to another dimension. When he wore his Dress Blues, he acted as if he was Superior to me.

White Hat – He was the overseer of my life.

Khaki Shirt – With Pleats, Straight and Firm, that laid against my cinnamon-colored body that ached from his abusive hands.

Khaki Belt w/Buckle – Were wrapped around my wrists or ankles so I would not run or fight.

Black shoes – Kicked or stomped me as I lay on the floor after being knocked down by him.

Blue Trousers w/Red Stripe – Blue and Black Bruises on my body and the blood I shed from his fists or vigorous sex.

White T-shirt – Worn underneath his shirt. I used it to wipe the tears from my eyes, blood from my lips or his tainted sperm from between my thighs.

Black Socks – Stuffed in my mouth so no one would hear my cries and or tie my hands or feet so I couldn't run.

White Briefs – Pulled out his penis from the hole to rape me.

Chapter 16
GRAIN OF COURAGE AND OUNCE OF STRENGTH

Throughout the years of being abused, I continuously heard my inner voice say "No more beatings! Enough is Enough!" After being abused, I always asked myself the million-dollar question, "Why do I stay?" The simple answer was I stayed because I was a young, inexperienced Mother and bride and had no sense of financial security and no means to acquire any. Over the years, I kept hearing my Mother's voice, echoing, "Stay because Mitch is a good husband and a good father "She was half right." I stayed because I was afraid, Mitch manipulated and controlled my mind so much that I couldn't think rationally and was mentally drained and physically pained. I had no self-esteem, no self-identity, and no self-worth after being sodomized and beaten – which stripped me of my pride and dignity. One day I woke up and could see clearly and could think clearly about my future.

Maybe it was the flashbacks I had of my black eyes; maybe it was the bruises on my face; maybe it was the scars on my back; maybe it was the marks on my buttocks; maybe it was the sunflower-shaped mirror that hung on my wall. When I took a good look at it, I convinced myself, "You are worthy" – and finally believed it; maybe it was the pain in my severed heart. I had lost the ability to nurture myself through those years of Abuse. I had to believe I was a worthy person to find my COURAGE AND STRENGTH. I found that

GRAIN OF COURAGE the size of a MUSTARD SEED and an OUNCE OF STRENGTH that awarded me the DETERMINATION to say "No More and Walked Away." I found them in my children's beautiful brown eyes when they gleamed at me that told me: *"Mother, if you can't find the STRENGTH to survive for yourself, find the COURAGE to survive for us!" We love you, we need you. Now and in our Futures"*

If you can find a Grain of Courage or an Ounce of Strength that's all it takes – to walk away from your abusive spouse or intimate partner, #GETOUTNOW!

The only day I wasn't beaten was a

day that didn't end in Y.

Sunday

Monday

Tuesday

Wednesday

Thursday

Friday

Saturday

The only month I wasn't beaten was a month that didn't end with a vowel or a consonant.

January
February
March
April
May
June
July
August
September
October
November
December

Chapter 17
YOU WORE IT WELL
(Custom Fit Dress)

Please design me a simple custom fit dress with these unique specifications:

The collar has to fold up past my forehead to cover my black eyes and the bruises on my face.

Let my hair flow down, since hair is a woman's glory. I never thought I would live to tell my story.

The sleeves must be long enough to cover the bruises on my arms.

I want my hands and fingers to be exposed because one day God might bless me with a Boaz to put a ring on my finger.

The dress has to be long enough so no one will see the bruises on my legs or the sores on my knees from crawling away.

I want my feet to show to remind me that God allowed me to walk away.

Don't forget the two holes for my eyes because I still need to see the footprints to my Destiny to which God is bringing me.

Don't forget the two holes for my ears so I can hear God's voice telling me "I never left you nor will I forsake you, my child!"

Leave a hole for my nose so I can breathe the air you tried to beat out of me.

Leave an opening for my mouth so I can tell women that are still being abused to #GetOutNow.

The top open part of the dress will remind me that the abuse that I endured for so many years…is over!

The dress must have a zipper down the back to remind me that the abuse is behind me now and it has come to an end.

The dress must be purple to remind me of God's Royalty, it's my favorite color, and the purple bruises that covered my face and body are no longer there.

Most importantly, it has to be a size 16 that's when I said "I do" and I made it through different levels of Abuse for 16 years.

If you are a Woman and a victim of physical, sexual, psychological and emotional abuse: this dress is NOT a One Size Fit All. All magnitudes (black eyes, bruises, scars, rape, and a shattered heart) are incomparable Abuse.

You best believe this dress will not be designed with spandex or any adjustments, whereas there will not be any alterations in my life to fit you or another abuser.

"You Wore it Well" "We Wore It Well"

Chapter 18
Resources for Victims of Physical and Sexual Abuse
(Military and Civilians)

If you are Military or Spouse of Military and you are a victim of spousal abuse or intimate Partner abuse, please contact your spouse's command.

The National Task Force to End Sexual and Domestic Violence Against Women began working on draft content for the Violence Against Women Act reauthorization. The Military Committee began its work by reviewing the following documents for relevancy in addressing current concerns. The task force report is posted on the Defense Domestic Violence Task Force.

The Violence Against Women Act: Background for Military Committee

www.dtic.mil/domesticviolence/index.htm.

Military One Source 800.342.9647

OCONUS Calling Options

https://www.miLittlearyonesource.mil/family-relationships/relationships/relationship-challenges-and-divorce/how-to-find-help-for-victims-of-domestic-abuse

Family Advocacy Program - Contact your Military Installation

Victim Advocate - Contact your Military Installation

Chaplain - Contact your Military Installation

Civilians - Please contact your local police

department - 911

The National Domestic Violence Hotline

1.800.799.7233   1.800.787.3224 (TTY)

https://www.thehotline.org/

RAINN SEXUAL ASSAULT

1.800.656.HOPE (4673)

www.rainn.org/CARE?utm_source=homepage&utm

_medium=web&utm_campaign=bystanderinterventi

on2019

National Suicide Prevention Hotline 800.273.8255

https://suicidepreventionlifeline.org/

Statistics on Domestic Violence In The Military And Civilian Communities

DEFENSE TASK FORCE ON DOMESTIC

VIOLENCE IN THE MILITARY

The Defense Task Force on Domestic Violence, in its 2001 report, made it clear that services to prevent the ongoing escalation of domestic violence in military families were insufficient. It made over two hundred suggestions to improve both the quality and the quantity of the military families response to domestic violence. It recommended that the Department of Defense require the investigation of every reported incident of domestic violence. When subsequent investigations were conducted, they revealed precisely what the kindling conditions are for domestic violence explosions. The report stated that these factors must be explored in depth if the epidemic is to take a downturn. The risk factors include previous conviction(s), prior head injury exacerbated by military service, and observable patterns of traumatic reenactment. Treating at-risk individuals before they reunite with their families provides critical protection.

In 2002, five women at Ft. Bragg in North Carolina were murdered by their Special Forces husbands who had just returned from combat in Afghanistan, drawing national attention to the issue of the rising rates of domestic violence in military families. Each of the killers was already known to be at risk because of prior domestic violence or similar behavior. Additionally, documented case studies that point to traumatic repetition are recorded in books such as T. S. Nelson's For Love of Country and Ed Tick's Sacred Mountain. By documenting the continuing impact of domestic violence within military families and pointing to traumatic reactivation as the causative factor, hope is engendered that families and children will be better served. Stories of how domestic violence plays out in the lives of military families are not intended to shock or cause despair but to evoke an understanding of how War does not end when it is declared over, and how the battles do not end when the soldiers come home.

Suggested Reading: *When War Comes Home: Christ Centered Healing For Wives of Combat Veterans* (Bridges to Healing Series), Ghrist Adsit, Rahnella Adsit and Marshelle Carter Waddell, 2008.

BLUE STAR FAMILY SURVEY ON DOMESTIC VIOLENCE

It's also a time to shine a light on domestic violence in the military and civilian communities. In recognition of Domestic Violence Awareness month, here is what our 2017 annual Military Family Lifestyle Survey (#BSFSurvey) says about how military and veteran families are affected by this issue. Fifteen percent of military and veteran family respondents in the 2017 #BSF Survey reported they did not feel physically safe in their relationship and a 2013 Virginia study found that approximately 22 percent of service members were Intimate Partner Violence (IPV) perpetrators.

In 2017, 87 percent of military spouse

respondents did not report their physical abuse citing their top two reasons for not reporting the abuse was because **they felt it was not a big deal** and because **they did not want to hurt their spouse or partner's career**. This percentage was even higher among veteran spouse respondents with 91 percent indicating they did not report their physical abuse citing their top reason as **they felt embarrassed**. Though few veterans and service member respondents indicated they had themselves been victims, of those who had, only 84 percent of veterans and no service members had reported the incident. For these populations, reasons for not reporting ranged from **fearing they would lose financial support or benefits to feeling it was not a big deal for lack of confidentiality to fear for their own career.**

(The task force report is posted on the Defense Domestic Violence Task Force Web site at www.dtic.mil/domesticviolence/index.htm.)

DOMESTIC VIOLENCE IN THE MILITARY

In 2002, there were more than 18,000 incidents of spousal abuse reported to the Department of Defense's Family Advocacy Program 84% of these incidents involved physical abuse. (U.S. Department of Defense, Family Advocacy Program Report: "Child and Spouse Abuse Data," FY97- 01.)

- Domestic violence victims in military communities are most likely to be women. 66% of cases identified female victims. (U.S.

Department of Defense, Family Advocacy Program Data, FY02.) 62% of abusers are on active military duty. (Child and Spouse Abuse Data, FY97-01.)

- Among active duty military women, 30% reported an adult lifetime prevalence of intimate partner abuse, while 22% reported intimate partner violence during military service. (Campbell, Garza, et al., Intimate Partner Violence and Abuse Among Active Duty Military Women, Violence Against Women, 2003.)

- Domestic Violence homicides in the military community from 1995-2001 include: 54 in the Navy or Marine Corps; 131 in the Army; 32 in the Air Force. (Initial Report of the Defense Task Force on Domestic Violence, U.S. Department of Defense, 2001.)

- In 2002, 24% of women surveyed by the Defense Department reported experiencing sexual harassment in the forms of crude/offensive behavior, unwanted sexual attention, and/or sexual coercion. (Armed Forces 2002 Sexual Harassment Survey, U.S. Department of Defense, 2001.)

- Although data is hard to obtain, it is apparent that relatively few military personnel are prosecuted or administratively sanctioned on charges stemming from domestic violence. (Initial Report of the Defense Task Force on Domestic Violence, U.S. Department of Defense, 2001.)

- The Department of Defense (DOD) divides the severity of abuse into three categories: severe physical abuse, moderate physical abuse, and mild physical abuse. The DOD severity definitions are inconsistent with commonly "characterizations" of domestic violence. A DOD prerequisite to be categorized as severe physical abuse is major physical injury requiring inpatient medical treatment or causing temporary or permanent disability or disfigurement. A strangulation case in the civilian community is considered very dangerous, whereas in the Department of Defense, it might be defined to be mild or moderate abuse. As a result 69% of domestic violence cases reported in FY99 were mild and only 6% were classified as severe. (Defense Task Force on Domestic Violence, 2003 Third Year Report," U.S. Department of Defense, February 2003.)

- In a 2001 Department of Defense memo on the subject of domestic violence, Deputy Defense Secretary Paul Wolfowitz declared, "domestic violence will not be tolerated in the Department of Defense." He made clear that "commanders at every level have a duty to take appropriate steps to prevent domestic violence, protect victims and hold those who commit it accountable." (Paul Wolfowitz, Deputy Secretary of Defense, Department of Defense Memo, November 19, 2001.)

- In spite of this memo, the rates of moderate and severe spousal abuse have increased between FY 1997-2001 (23% to 36% for moderate, 2% to 7% for severe). Mild spousal abuse, on the other hand, has decreased (72% to 57%). (U.S. Department of Defense, Family Advocacy Program

Report: "Child and Spouse Abuse Data," FY97-01.)

- According to Defense Secretary Donald Rumsfeld, "Domestic violence is a pervasive problem that transcends all ethnic, racial, gender and socioeconomic boundaries, and it will not be tolerated in the Department of Defense. Domestic violence destroys individuals, ruins families and weakens our communities. (Department of Defense Memo, April 2001 in response to the Initial Report of the Defense Task Force on Domestic Violence.)

TRANSITIONAL COMPENSATION: HELP FOR VICTIMS OF ABUSE

Victims of abuse can feel isolated and discouraged. For the families of military service members, this isolation can be more intense when living far from extended family and close friends. If you've bravely decided to leave an abusive relationship, transitional compensation is a financial benefit that can help you move and get back on your feet. To be eligible for the benefit: A dependent-abuse offense must be listed as a reason for the separation or forfeiture, although it does not have to be the primary reason. Active duty victims of domestic violence are also eligible for transitional compensation, when the offender is also active duty.

Amount of the benefit: The compensation amount is based on the Dependency and Indemnity Compensation, which changes annually. Current amounts can be found at the Department of Veterans Affairs Dependency and Indemnity Compensation website.

Transitional compensation is one of the many resources available to you as a victim of domestic abuse.

Your installation's Family Advocacy Program or legal assistance office can help you apply for transitional compensation and provide you additional information on legal topics such as divorce.

National Statistics for Non-Military

9 in 10 Adults Say Family Violence is a Much Bigger Problem than Most People Think

Nine in ten adults (92 percent) say that family violence is a much bigger problem than most people think, and 89 percent regard it as a form of domestic terrorism. A new survey conducted for Family Circle and Lifetime Television finds that nine in ten Americans say that verbal abuse can do as much damage as physical abuse, and that a husband who forces himself on his wife is guilty of rape.

REFERENCES

Adults Say Family Violence is a Much Bigger Problem than Most People think. Retrieved (2020, March 10) http://www.ncdsv.org/images/9in10AdultsSayFamily ViolenceMuchBiggerProble.pdf

Brach, T. (2011). Retrieved from (2020, March 10)https://trauma-recovery.ca/introduction/definition-of-trauma/

Center for Disease Control Statistics and Domestic Violence. Retrieved (2020, March 10). https://www.google.com/search?q=cdc+statistics+on+domestic+violence&rlz=1C1CHBF_enUS850US8

52&oq=cdcstatitics+on+domestic+&aqs=chrome.1.

69i57j0.12543j0j4&sourceid=chrome&ie=UTF-8

Domestic Violence in Military Families Retrieved

(2020, March 10) http://criminal-

justice.iresearchnet.com/crime/domestic-

violence/military-families/

Here's what Military Families say about Domestic

Violence. Retrieved (2020, March 10)

https://bluestarfam.org/2018/10/heres-what-military-

spouses-say-about-domestic-violence/

National Coalition Against Domestic Violence.

Retrieved (2020, March 10)

https://ncadv.org/statistics

Relationship Challenges and Divorce. Retrieved

(2020, March 10) https://www.onesource.mil/family-relationships/relationships/relationships-challenges-

and-divorce/transitional-compensation-help-for-

victims-of-abuse

Rockefeller, J. (2018). Retrieved (2020, March 10)

https://breakthesilencedv.org/dealing-with-triggers-

after-domestic-violence/

Made in the USA
Columbia, SC
29 October 2020